www.finder.com/cryptocurrency

WHAT IS CRYPTOCURRENCY

Your complete guide to bitcoin, blockchain and beyond

Written By: *Chris Stead*

www.finder.com/cryptocurrency

Second Edition – 2018

Written and Designed by: Chris Stead

Sub-Editor: David Gregory

Global Crypto Finder team: Andrew Munro, Harry Tucker, James Edwards and Tim Falk

Producers: Molly Wiltshire-Bridle and Angus Kidman

Legal and Compliance: Sean Graham

ISBN-13: 978-1-925638-18-9

CONTENTS

DISCLAIMER

The information presented in this book should not be interpreted as an endorsement of cryptocurrency or any specific provider, service or offering. It is not a recommendation to trade. Cryptocurrencies are speculative, complex and involve significant risks – they are highly volatile and sensitive to secondary activity. Performance is unpredictable and past performance is no guarantee of future performance. Consider your own circumstances, and obtain your own advice, before relying on this information. You should also verify the nature of any product or service (including its legal status and relevant regulatory requirements) and consult the relevant Regulators' websites before making any decision. The writers at finder may have holdings in the cryptocurrencies discussed.

The information in this book is accurate as of October 2018.

I. INTRODUCTION

Cryptocurrencies aren't future technology. They're already being used today, and they're doing things that were impossible just a few short years ago. Imagine sending US dollars to Australia, having it automatically converted to Australian dollars and deposited in the account of your choice. Now imagine doing it almost instantly and anonymously, at competitive exchange rates, all while paying just a couple of dollars or less in fees.

That's not a hypothetical example. That's something you could do today if you wanted, and it's just the tip of the iceberg. It's all made possible by a technology called blockchain. It's a technology that allows information to be encrypted and then stored, accessed and transferred between individuals

Most cryptocurrencies are built for a specific purpose and with the specific intention of being able to do a task better than anything else that's come before it. It has expanded well beyond the concept of simply transferring finances and has expanded into every industry, from politics and medicine to music and manufacturing. This makes them the perfect disruptors of existing industries.

Despite being around since 2009, cryptocurrency burst into the mainstream in 2017. Over the course of the year, the total value of the cryptocurrency market rose from US$18 billion to US$796 billion, an increase of US$778 billion. By comparison, the total value rose just US$11 billion in 2016. Alongside this boom, the number of cryptocurrencies has drastically risen, with over 1500 altcoins now joining the famous bitcoin on the trading room floor.

In this guide, we'll help take you from interested rookie to master trader by providing you with foundational knowledge required to understand cryptocurrency. Note: At the back of this book you will find a glossary of terms, so if you encounter a word you don't understand, be sure to reference this section for more guidance.

Who is Crypto Finder?

Before we dive deep into the world of cryptocurrency, let's answer a question about the logo you no doubt saw on the front cover or on the title page. What is Crypto Finder? Crypto Finder is part of the finder.com family, the brand through which finder provides information, news and analysis about cryptocurrencis, tokens and related matters.

Finder is one of the world's leading comparison websites. An award-winning fintech company, our goal is to help people around the world make better financial decisions and improve their lives.

Here at finder, we compare financial products including credit cards, savings accounts, home loans, personal loans, online shopping discount and codes, travel insurance and life insurance. But we also compare energy, mobile phones, Internet service providers, video games and plenty more. Crypto Finder refers to the subsection of the website focusing on comparing the cryptocurrency market.

We understand that making everyday life decisions can be quite daunting. That's why we're here. We help you navigate those complex decisions by making them less of a chore (and hopefully less of a bore, too!).

finder is privately owned and self-funded, starting out in Australia in 2006. It is now the most visited personal finance comparison website in Australia and we're launching around the world, with offices in Sydney (Australia), New York City (USA), London (UK), Manila (Philippines) and Wroclaw (Poland).

Our service is proudly free to use! We don't sell your information to marketers or harass you with annoying phone calls. Plus, we don't mark up prices or apply additional fees. We're on your side!

Inside this extensive guide, you will find all the base knowledge and know-how you need to approach the cryptocurrency market feeling empowered. However, it is to be considered as a complement to, and foundational read for, the activity occurring on the finder website.

For the very latest news and up-to-date comparisons, check the website. You may also want to consider signing up to the website.

What is Crypto Finder TV

For those who like to keep abreast of the developments in cryptocurrency through the video format, there's a whole suite of shows to enjoy via Crypto Finder TV.

Crypto Finder is your guide to everything to do with crypto, blockchain and distributed ledger — and comes from the writers and analysts behind global finance comparison website, **finder.com**. Each day, our team produce researched guides, market analysis, reviews, comparison, interviews, news, video and podcasts. Our mission: to help you make better informed decisions.

That goal now sees Crypto Finder content published across 18 countries and also translated into several languages.

Our lineup of shows, interviews and video guides can be watched live (or on demand) across YouTube, Facebook, Twitch and Twitter — and here at **cryptofinder.tv**. We love answering your questions on air!

You can also watch on your big screen TV (from your phone) using Apple AirPlay or Google Chromecast and subscribe to Crypto Finder's regular podcasts using your favourite apps like iTunes, Stitcher or Soundcloud.

II. IT ALL STARTED WITH BITCOIN

The road to current boom in cryptocurrency started in the 1980s. In an effort to protect the cash of small shops and gas stations, banks began investigating and pushing the idea of points of sale, where a customer could use a credit card instead of cash to pay for products.

Later, in the 90s, came a web-based payment system still used today: PayPal. This gave merchants the power to accept credit card payments online and it introduced the idea of transferring fiat currencies, the traditional money of a country, directly between end users entirely online. With PayPal proving that the web is a viable medium for transferring currency, similar services were created, such as WebMoney (a Russian PayPal alternative) and e-Gold, an American corporation that let users buy gold online – gold that it would then hold on a customer's behalf.

In the 2000s, after the FBI shut down e-Gold, cryptocurrencies began popping up in the cryptography community and through mailing lists. Known as the Cypherpunks, people like Julian Assange, the famous founder of WikiLeaks, and Jacob Appelbaum, the developer of Tor, were notable members of this underground movement.

Unfortunately, none of these cryptocurrencies could gather the necessary momentum to push them into the public's consciousness until, in 2008, Satoshi Nakamoto published a paper titled "Bitcoin: A Peer-to-Peer Electronic Cash System."

In it, Satoshi – whose real identity remains unknown (we don't even know if Satoshi is an individual or a group) – detailed a system for decentralizing the financial sector, with the aim of giving power back to the people via an entirely digital transaction system. This would later become known as the blockchain. In January 2009, the first block of the bitcoin blockchain was mined by Satoshi, for which he (she? it?) was awarded 50 bitcoin.

In the years to come, bitcoin grew to become not only the number one cryptocurrency available on the market, but is established as a household name among even those who have no interest in cryptocurrencies.

Bitcoin eventually gave rise to hundreds of cryptocurrencies, known collectively as altcoins. Some of these altcoins are little more than copies of bitcoin, but others are attempting to do things with the underlying blockchain technology that not only disrupt the financial sector but also our understanding of apps and website services in an attempt to fix today's problem of centralization. While still directly involved in the development of bitcoin, Satoshi is rumored to have mined nearly one million bitcoin, an amount that would, just nine years later, be worth upwards of US$5.8 billion.

The problem with centralization

Read any literature relating to bitcoin and cryptocurrencies and you'll eventually stumble upon the concept of decentralization. To understand decentralization, you first need to understand the problem with centralization.

If we take a close look at the world we inhabit today, a world of information and data about who we are, what we do, and what we like, we realize that our information is held by a few large organizations: private and public corporations as well as the government. The dataset representing you (financial records, emails, Facebook messages and likes, etc.) is held on servers that exist in a central location. For example, your financial records, every transaction you've ever been a part of, your current balance and all your loans, exist on your bank's servers. Your bank might have multiple servers for backup and audit purposes, but it still all exists in virtually one location: your bank.

So let's say a malicious hacker, also known as a cracker, attacks your bank's servers and tampers with your account reducing your balance to $0. How can you prove that you didn't just withdraw all your money? How can your bank verify your claim that you were hacked?

The Cypherpunks, the community from which cryptocurrencies first arose, understood this bleak scenario and aimed to fix it. Cryptocurrencies are said to be decentralized systems because every user of a cryptocurrency keeps a copy of everyone's transaction history. The moment you join a blockchain, you receive the entire history of that cryptocurrency. In other words, you get a copy of all transactions ever made with that cryptocurrency. If a user disagrees with a transaction (say a hacker changes their wallet value from 1 BTC to 1,000 BTC) a consensus must be reached by at least 51% of the users of that cryptocurrency. That 51% then decides what the correct amount should be.

This automatic consensus is the beauty behind cryptocurrencies and decentralization. There is no one server that crackers can attack. They would need to hack 51% of all users because every user keeps a copy of the blockchain.

The problem with decentralization

The early 2017 struggles of the 0x Protocol (ZRX) highlight the overlooked challenges of decentralization. 0x (ZRX) is a system designed specifically for decentralized ERC20 exchanges such as Paradex and Ethfinex. A decentralized exchange is one in which all the transactions are undertaken on a blockchain, as opposed to a centralized exchange such as Binance. The benefit to this approach is that it's near impossible for a decentralized exchange to be hacked and funds stolen. However, the 0x Protocol also highlighted its downsides - namely, the speed on which transfers can occur, and the often complex nature of the user experience. Like many other cryptocurrencies it's part currency, part open-source software project and part social experiment.

That third element can be tricky. Power and wealth have a natural tendency to consolidate (the "trickle up" effect) because the more power and wealth one group has, the easier it is to accrue even more. In cryptocurrency, this can be a major problem. An imbalanced coin risks losing function and value, and in more immediate terms, the actual security of decentralized ledgers is dependent on maintaining a certain balance.

Where a coin's functionality develops only by democratic vote, too much power in one bloc can also have lasting effects. For example, Bitcoin Cash and Bitcoin Gold were created mostly by accident through power struggles in the bitcoin community. The different blocs, such as the miners and the holders, each tried to change the programming to suit their needs, but couldn't get enough support to pull it off cleanly.

As a result, they split off from the bitcoin community to create their own coins. Arguably the remaining bitcoin core faction is left with a fanatical purist bent, which is having its own long-term effects.

Coins need to find a system that enables, and maintains, a suitable level of decentralization and not just for freedom, fairness and democracy. There are critical functional and economic reasons to find a balance that works. For example, a central overarching power can help market a coin, form partnerships, deal with any compliance or legal issues that arise across countries and ensure roadmap goals are met.

Different cryptocurrencies approach this challenge in different ways. For example, Ripple foregoes decentralization entirely; ARK uses a democratically elected council of 51 very well paid programming elders; and IOTA installed a temporary coordinator to keep it safe until it turns into an all grown up decentralized Tangle network.

The 0x Protocol is currently trying out a bit of social engineering. It is being designed to give both the "relayers" and the "traders" a say in the development of the system.

Relayers: The people who run off-chain nodes to conduct decentralized exchange (DEX) transactions. Basically, they carry out DEX transactions and collect fees in ZRX for all of their work.

Traders: These are the people who buy and sell cryptocurrencies (and maybe other things someday) via the relayers. Decentralized exchanges such as Paradex, IDEX, Waves Dex would fall into this group.

Naturally, only ZRX token holders get to have a say in the development of the system. This ensures that the voters have a reasonable vested interest and helps prevent manipulation. The challenge is actually vesting that interest in an appropriate balance of parties and making sure it lasts. Left to its own devices in its barest form, control of the 0x Protocol (in the form of ZRX holdings) would tend to migrate in the direction of the relayers. And over time, 0x would then develop to best suit the relayers rather than the traders. This kind of imbalance isn't sustainable.

The solution is to make sure traders will continue to maintain a suitable stake in the system and make their voices heard – even if they don't necessarily want to. In the case of 0x, this is done by requiring heavy traders to hold a certain amount of ZRX tokens before they can access the 0x functions and by using ZRX as a fee token.

The good news is that this naturally ensures that traders will continue to get a vote and maintain balance in the system. The bad news is that it comes at a very literal cost. Buying the required stake isn't always cheap, and few people would willingly pay fees if they don't have to. 0x co-founder Will Warren described the problem in a Reddit post.

"We want to avoid a situation where the only people participating in governance are relayers because (1) this isn't very decentralized and (2) because relayers are running for-profit businesses and their incentives do not necessarily align with their end users. It is critical that decentralized governance is run by all groups of stakeholders in the 0x ecosystem; relayers and traders. By requiring traders (or at least heavy traders) to hold some amount of ZRX tokens to access 0x Protocol's functionality via relayers, they will have a vested interest in ensuring 0x Protocol evolves in a way that satisfies their needs."

However, there is an ongoing problem with this solution, which cryptocurrency makers continue to debate. How much tax would you pay if it were an optional donation? Decentralized governance might be an essential part of a system, but it's not a feature that most people will willingly pay for. As an added cost, it can inhibit uptake of a coin and undermine the system in a different way.

III. THE BLOCKCHAIN

Cryptocurrencies are digital tokens that have a value, just like a $10 note is a physical token that happens to have a value of $10. The problem with digital currencies is that they're purely electronic. Just like a photograph on the Internet can be copied and replicated over and over again until the original is worthless, the same thing could happen to a coin.

In order for a cryptocurrency to have value, a coin needs to be unique and impossible to replicate. This was made possible by the invention of blockchain technology. A blockchain is simply a ledger that contains the entire history of all transactions made with a certain cryptocurrency. By tracking all the movements and the entire history of a currency, it's impossible to make any counterfeits. To prevent tampering, most blockchains are open source and decentralized, which creates trust.

Open source: The programming is made publicly available, so anyone can see exactly how it works. This prevents tampering from inside sources.

Decentralized: The primary feature of the blockchain is that it's a decentralized, distributed database of transactions. The most common way of storing such transactions today is using a single database stored on a central server. For example, all your banking transactions are stored on a central database on a server belonging to your bank. If this database were hacked, the bank might have a backup database to compare the data and revert back to the original, but what if that backup was also hacked? How many backups of the database would an organization have to keep, and maintain, in order to be safe?

Blockchains are operated by different people connected from all around the world. With public blockchains such as bitcoin, anyone can start operating a node, a computer linked to the bitcoin network, on the blockchain whenever they want. As there are thousands of independent nodes randomly scattered around the world all hosting the entire history of transactions, it prevents any single individual or group of individuals from taking over the network. If one user were to tamper with the data, all the other copies would disagree and flag that one copy of the ledger as corrupt, and it would be ignored. You'd have to change 51% of the nodes in exactly the same way at exactly the same time. This prevents tampering from outside sources.

Trust: The transparent and immutable nature of the blockchain also solves the problem of trust. There is no third party that you need to trust with your data, no central bank or government, no organization or for-profit business. All transactions that are stored on the blockchain and broadcast to every single user of the blockchain, and you hold a copy of that same ledger

Why is it called a blockchain?

The name blockchain refers to the particular way it assembles data in the ledger. Each block is like a container for transactions. These transactions are recorded in a block as data, and this data usually includes the wallet address of the coin sender and receiver as well as the amount sent. When you make a transaction that is confirmed by all the nodes as being legitimate (e.g., you're not trying to copy a coin that already exists), this information is packed into the block. Once the transaction is added to a block, it cannot be edited or removed. This ensures the security and reliable of the blockchain.

When a block is ready to go, it's added to the blockchain. This is like having a signed and sealed package sent off to be recorded.

Each block is digitally strung together like the links of metal in a chain. It's attached to the one that comes before it and the one that comes after, creating an unbroken and tamper-proof history of every single transaction executed in the history of the cryptocurrency. Each block is given a number, and anyone can look back and see the transactions that were carried on each block.

As of the start of 2018, there have been roughly 500,000 blocks in the history of bitcoin. But it's important to note that in general, each cryptocurrency has its own blockchain. So there is a bitcoin blockchain, an Ethereum blockchain, a Ripple blockchain and so forth, each recording the transactions occurring in their own ecosystem.

Most blockchains are simply one unbroken chain. But others are more complicated and might run other chains off the side of the main blockchain, or they might try assembling blocks in a web-like structure rather than a single chain. Not all blockchains work exactly the same, and not all cryptocurrencies even use a blockchain. But the basic principles and their implications remain the same.

While initially intended to be a public ledger for bitcoin transactions, many cryptocurrencies today are pushing this technology to the limit, and its adoption has been explored by governments, financial institutions and many other industries.

In summary, the blockchain has four primary advantages over other means of tracking the ownership of a digital product:

- It is not, and cannot, be controlled by a single entity.*

- It has no single point of failure.

- Transactions are embedded in the network and held by everyone who is using the blockchain.

- Altering information on the blockchain would require tampering with the entire network at once.

* The notable exception to this is if enough entities group together in order to attain 51% control over the network. This is very rare, but can happen.

A case study

When a transaction occurs, it happens between two entities that hold a unique digital address. This is an encrypted key, which is more colloquially termed a wallet. Amy has a wallet, and in her wallet she has 0.001 bitcoin that also has its own unique address. Amy wants to sell 0.001 bitcoin, and Bob wants to buy 0.001 bitcoin. This transaction request is broadcast to the network of bitcoin users and asks, "Does Amy's unique wallet address hold that particular 0.001 bitcoin fraction?"

This transaction (along with a set amount of other recent transactions) is validated via a process known as mining. The miners, the individuals who own the nodes (read: computers) on the network, will compare the digital signature unique to that 0.001 bitcoin with the historical ledger. If a consensus is reached by multiple nodes that the wallet owned by Amy does indeed hold that particular 0.001 bitcoin, then the transaction to Bob can be confirmed. This transaction then becomes a block. This block is then appended to the end of the existing blockchain in a way that's permanent and immutable (i.e., it cannot be edited or deleted).

The future of the blockchain

While initially designed to support bitcoin, there have been many exciting developments based on the blockchain.

Finance: Blockchain's biggest draw at the turn of 2018 remains in the finance sector. Banks and financial institutions have been heavily investing time and money into researching potential ways the blockchain could help improve the way they do business. Nearly instantaneous transactions, nationally or across borders, and in-built verification would cut out a lot of middlemen.

Decentralized data: In the same way that the blockchain decentralizes the database of transactions for bitcoin and other altcoins, it could be used to store any type of data. Startups have been investigating the idea of using the blockchain to store data and big data from applications in the same distributed and secure fashion.

Smart contracts: Developed by Ethereum, smart contracts are programmable contracts that stay on the blockchain until the conditions specified in the contract are met. Once they are, the contract automatically executes the transaction it was programmed to execute. For example, a smart contract can be developed to send a specified amount of bitcoin to a particular wallet on a specific day of every month (e.g., to pay rent automatically). Smart contracts enjoy the same immutability features of normal transactions.

Governance: Because of the completely transparent nature of the blockchain, any sort of poll-taking (for example, national elections) would benefit greatly from being stored on blockchain technology. Once a vote has been made, the transaction would be verified and then validated automatically, and stored on the blockchain for everyone to see, tamper-proof and permanent.

Land title registration: The blockchain makes any sort of record keeping more efficient, while being publicly accessible makes it fully transparent. With their susceptibility to fraud and the high cost of labor required to maintain them, property titles are a perfect candidate for the blockchain. The move to blockchain has been adopted by a few governments already, including Honduras (2015) and the Republic of Georgia (2017).

Remember, blockchain allows the digital transfer of anything of value, so this goes way beyond obvious applications like digital currencies. Potential applications also being explored include the following:

- Peer-to-peer payments

- International money transfers

- Transferring ownership of equities and clearing settlements

- Patient health-records management

- Digitally recorded property assets like media

- Proof of ownership for digital content

- Monetization of data

IV. UNDERSTANDING MINING

In order for a cryptocurrency to exist, it needs to be mined and the people who do this are miners. Miners confirm blocks on the blockchain and should not be confused with people underground with pickaxes. The following explanation focuses on bitcoin, since it's the hero coin of the cryptocurrency market, but it's important to note that cryptocurrencies differ in the technology behind how their blockchains work – most notably in the way the algorithm that encrypts the data operates. But the base concept remains interchangeable.

Unlike regular fiat currencies (such as US dollars, Australian dollars or euros), cryptocurrency assets are not controlled by a central government or bank, and new cryptocurrency (be it bitcoin or an altcoin) cannot be printed and issued like paper money. Instead, bitcoin tokens are introduced into the market via a process known as "mining." New bitcoin tokens, or a fraction of a bitcoin token, are awarded to the miners who have solved the math problems necessary to verify bitcoin transactions.

As explained in the previous chapter, whenever a transaction is made in a cryptocurrency, a record of it is made on a block containing other recent transactions. Think of it as the same page in a traditional physical ledger. Once the block is full, the cryptocurrency's miners compete against each other to verify and validate the block and all its transactions against other nodes in the network by solving a complex cryptographic problem.

The first miner to accomplish this task is awarded a set amount of the cryptocurrency, based on the mining difficulty at the time. The verified block is then added to the blockchain, which is a history of all blocks that have been verified since the beginning of the cryptocurrency, and transmitted to all the nodes in that cryptocurrency's network so that they can have the latest version of the blockchain.

This cryptocurrency award to miners is not the only process by which new currency is added to the market, but it can become an income stream. This is because the cryptocurrency has value. However, the act of mining requires intense computer resources, which requires not only expensive hardware, but also a lot of energy.

This is because at the heart of cryptocurrency mining lies a hard, mathematical problem. The goal is to ensure that the process of adding a new block to the blockchain requires a lot of work. That helps to ensure that any hacker tampering with the transactions needs to not only mess with the transactions, but to also win the "race" of being the winning miner when it comes to verifying the transaction.

How does mining work?

The blockchain is run by people's computers all over the world. In order to ensure the blockchain is running smoothly and reliably, and isn't tampered with, these computers, called nodes, need to solve math problems to show they're working. By doing this, they can prove they're a legitimate part of the network and doing what they should be.

The math problems, called mining algorithms, aren't particularly difficult. In fact, you could even do them with pen and paper. Instead, they're designed to be time-consuming to keep the blockchain ticking along at an appropriate speed, not too fast or too slow.

SHA-256 is the mining algorithm, which is the equation used to encrypt the cryptocurrency, used by bitcoin and it's a one-way cryptographic algorithm. Many cryptocurrencies can use the same algorithm. For example, many cryptocurrencies use ERC20, which is the algorithm instituted by Ethereum.

With bitcoin, when you pass a word through SHA-256, you will be given back an unrecognizable string of letters and numbers. This is called a hash. For example, the SHA-256 hash for the word BUTTERFLY is...

> 8c62ace4f9ef8ccd08ca6fb992a8524bb7dbdc0530654bd254c9da07a660949a.

This seemingly random string of letters and numbers has three important properties:

1. Only the word BUTTERFLY will ever give that specific hash.

2. The word BUTTERFLY will always give back that exact hash.

3. There is no way of figuring out the word BUTTERFLY if you only know the hash.

With this information, we can now start piecing together the mining process. Generally, and certainly with bitcoin, mining involves three variables: the block, the mining difficulty and a random number. Here's how it all comes together.

Imagine our block consists of the word BUTTERFLY as discussed earlier. In reality, the block would contain a list of recent, unverified transactions, but let's keep it simple in this example. In order for the block to be solved, bitcoin uses a deceptively simple test: If the hash result of the block starts with a certain number of zeros, the block is considered verified. This number of zeros is the "mining difficulty" and is increased as more miners join the bitcoin network. For our example, let's say that we have a mining difficulty of just two, so our hash must start with two zeros.

The problem is that BUTTERFLY will always return the exact same hash, and it doesn't start with two zeros. So what we need is the third variable, a random number (called a nonce).

We take this number, combine it with the word BUTTERFLY and hash again into a new string. If it doesn't start with two zeros, we change the number and try again. Because changing one small number changes the whole hash result, there is no way to predict the number we'll need to solve this!

We repeat this process over and over until we find a number that, when combined with the word BUTTERFLY, gives us a hash that starts with two zeros. That number is the solution to the block. This arduous process of randomly trying to find a number that gives the solution is what makes bitcoin mining such a computationally expensive process, and as more miners join the network, the harder it gets.

As of the turn of 2018, a regular home computer working alone, that is, not an application-specific integrated circuit (ASIC) and not part of a cloud mining network, would take 2.7 million years to mine one block.

This has led to the rise of ASIC computers built specifically for mining and to an increase in cloud mining. It's also led to an upsurge in the purchase of graphics cards that can lend computation weight to mining, which has created shortages around the world.

For a miner to receive their reward for lending their computational power to "solving" a block of transactions so it can be verified and added to the blockchain, they must provide some sort of proof they were involved. For bitcoin and many other altcoins, they must provide what is called proof of work.

Proof of work (PoW): This is how the miner shows that their computer contributed effort to approve a transaction. This is noted by a variable, added to the process of hashing a transaction, which demands that some effort is required before a block can be successfully hashed. Having a hashed block proves the miner's computer did some work and deserves a reward – hence proof of work.

Other cryptocurrencies use variations of this concept.

Proof of stake (PoS): This caps the reward given to miners for providing their computational power to the network at that miner's holdings in the cryptocurrency. So if a miner holds three coins, they can only earn three coins. This system encourages miners to stick with a certain blockchain, rather than converting their rewards to an alternate cryptocurrency after it has been successfully mined.

Proof of authority (PoA): A private, encrypted key that gives the holder the right to create the blocks in a private blockchain. It can be held by a single entity or a set number of entities. This is an alternative to the proof-of-work model since instead of getting multiple random nodes to approve a transaction, a group of specific nodes are given the authority to approve. This is a far faster method.

Do people make money mining cryptocurrencies?

The short answer is yes, but making money mining bitcoin and some of the other higher value cryptocurrencies is much more difficult today than it was in the industry's infancy. The following are some of the issues contributing to this difficulty:

Hardware prices: The days of mining using a standard central processing unit (CPU) or graphic card are gone. As more people have begun mining, the difficulty of solving the puzzles has increased. ASIC microchips were developed to process the computations faster and have become necessary to succeed at mining today. These chips can cost $3,000 or more and are guaranteed to further increase in cost with each improvement and update.

Rise in corporate miners: Hobby miners must now compete with for-profit organizations, and their bigger, better machines, when mining to make a buck.

Puzzle difficulty: Bitcoin's protocol adjusts the computational difficulty of the puzzles to finish a full block every 2,016 transaction blocks. The more computational power put toward mining, the more difficult the puzzle.

Power costs: Power in Western countries like Australia, the UK and the USA is more expensive than it is in other parts of the world, making it more difficult to compete with big-mining companies in the East.

It is the power costs that catch a lot of prospective miners off-guard. After all, we rarely consider how much power our electric appliances are consuming. But computing hashes is a very intensive process, pushing whatever processor you're using to the limit and to its maximum power consumption.

Also, cryptocurrency mining has changed as the industry has grown, requiring bigger and more expensive machines to successfully mine the more popular cryptocurrencies. The following is a quick history of the way cryptocurrency mining has changed as the industry and power requirements have grown.

CPU mining: In the early days of bitcoin, mining difficulty was low and not a lot of miners were competing for blocks and rewards. This made it worthwhile to use your computer's own CPU to mine bitcoin. However, that approach was soon replaced by GPU mining.

GPU mining: A graphics processing unit (GPU) is a powerful processor whose sole purpose is to assist your computer's graphics card in rendering 3D graphics. GPUs are not built for executive decisions (like CPUs), but are very good laborers, hence GPUs are able to execute over 800 times more instructions in the same amount of time as a CPU. Mining is a repetitive process that does not require any intelligent decisions, leading to GPUs replacing CPUs in the mining world.

FPGA mining: Next came mining with field-programmable gate arrays (FPGAs). These greatly outperformed GPUs and CPUs in the mining process as FPGAs are processors that can be programmed to execute specific instructions and only those instructions (instead of being repurposed for mining, like GPUs were).

ASIC mining: Similar to FPGAs, application-specific integrated circuits (ASIC) are chips designed for a specific purpose, in our case mining bitcoin, and nothing else. ASICs for bitcoin were introduced in 2013 and, as of the start of 2018, they are the best processors available for mining bitcoin and they outperform FPGAs in power consumption.

Mining pools: To offset the difficulty of mining a block, miners started organizing in pools or cloud-mining networks. Whenever a miner in one of these pools solves a block, the reward is shared with everyone in the pool in a ratio representative of how much work you put into the pool (even though you personally never solved the puzzle).

Cloud mining: The cloud offers prospective miners the ability to purchase mining rigs in a remote data center location. There are many advantages, the most obvious being no electricity costs, no excess heat and nothing to sell when you eventually decide to hang up your virtual pickaxe.

So which of these options will give you the best return once you factor in all of your energy costs? If you're using CPU/GPU/FPGA to mine, then you're unlikely to make money mining any of the major cryptocurrencies like bitcoin. While this may change, at the turn of 2018, the bitcoin reward is so small that it doesn't pay for the energy your computer will consume to verify a block.

This leaves us with pools, ASICs and cloud mining options. If you're not willing to put a lot of money into setting up a mining operation, your best bet could be to get a cloud mining rig. These are relatively low cost, require no hardware knowledge to get started, no extra electricity bills and you won't end up with a machine you can't sell when cryptocurrency mining is no longer profitable.

A new kind of virus

Mining can be a profitable source of revenue if you can do it on a serious scale, and this fact has opened up the digital world to a new kind of malicious attack. This includes viruses that infect a user's computer, which instead of stealing data, steal computing power. These viruses activate when you turn on the computer and hang around in the background, using some of your hardware power to mine a cryptocurrency, with the proceeds going to the hacker's wallet.

Privacy coins, which are altcoins that declare themselves to be truly anonymous, are the perfect target for these kinds of viruses. One suck virus is said to have infected over

15 million computers in late January 2018, using the victims' computer power to mine Monero. Security researchers at Palo Alto found that a large-scale cryptocurrency mining operation had been active for several months. The operation used the open-source XMRig tool, a malware that uses VBS (Visual Basic Scripting) files and various online URL shortening services, to install and run the XMRig payload.

Palo Alto said it found the malicious files were stored on 4sync's cloud storage and distributed by obfuscating filenames by using URL shortening services. Users were then duped into opening the files which, in turn, installed the malicious payloads. The malware used the NiceHash marketplace to sell the stolen processor power, harvested by the malware, to generate Monero cryptocurrency.

This isn't the first time Monero has been used by threat actors and criminals. In another recent crypto jacking operation, malware used YouTube ads to mine cryptocurrency using the computing resources of its victims.

If your computer starts running slowly, use a system utility like Activity Monitor on a Mac or Task Manager with Windows to check if your processor is getting thrashed when it should otherwise be idle. That may be a sign you've been crypto jacked.

If you're interested in learning more, a detailed, four part series on cryptocurrency mining can be found on the Finder Insights blog. In order to read it, just point your browser towards www.finder.com.au/crypto-mining-ultimate-guide.

V. THE
CRYPTOCURRENCY LOOP

So let's take a little recap; if you've been following along, you should have a good idea now of how the cryptocurrency loop works. The cryptocurrency loop refers to the way in which miners help uphold a coin's network, and in doing so, earn that coin as a payment. They therefore bring that new coin into the marketplace.

Here's a recap of this loop, starting at the beginning.

When a cryptocurrency is first created, a certain amount is released to the market. These could first go to traders or community members, and then to early adopters via an initial coin offering (ICO). The cryptocurrency's creators decide on a value for the cryptocurrency and then typically release a very limited amount during the ICO. Individuals who buy into an ICO generally do so because they see a use case for the cryptocurrencies blockchain that they believe will see its value increase when it hits the market.

For example, a particular cryptocurrency might claim that its blockchain tech may revolutionize digital media distribution.

The money raised during this ICO is used as the capital to bring the cryptocurrency's technology to fruition, as well as the cryptocurrency into the wider trading market. At this point, the coin's value will fluctuate based on market demand. As it is sold and bought, miners must confirm transactions and build blocks for the blockchain. As the miners confirm these transactions, they also create more of the cryptocurrency, which is then brought into the market.

This is what we call, the loop.

It's worth noting that not all cryptocurrencies have an infinite supply of coins to be mined; some are capped. This includes bitcoin, which is capped at 21 million. The aim is to create a greater value for each coin by ensuring there is a finite supply. Not all of those bitcoin are in the market as of 2018; in fact, the amount of bitcoin released to miners when a block is verified gets less each time, slowing the supply into the market with each passing month. It will drag on till 2140, which the algorithm has determined will be the likely moment that the last of the 21 million coins is awarded.

VI. EXPLAINING ICOS

ICO stands for "initial coin offering." It's a lot like an IPO (initial public offering) in traditional trading but for cryptocurrencies. Buying a successful cryptocurrency in its ICO stage can work out well, just like someone who bought a lot of shares in Apple, Microsoft or Google early became a millionaire later as the shares increased in value.

However, while the reward with ICOs can be great, the risk is significant. The U.S. Securities and Exchange Commission has identified that the vast majority of ICOs are frauds. This is an issue we will tackle later in the chapter.

Still, some of the biggest cryptocurrencies on the market started life as an ICO. For example, Ethereum began as an ICO, pitching its alternative use of blockchain technology focused on delivering smart contracts. Each Ethereum token was initially sold for 0.0005 bitcoin, but has multiplied around 200 times in value since then.

An ICO occurs when a company sells a new cryptocurrency coin to the public for the first time. It's designed to spread the new currency and to make sure it has plenty of traders. Later on, these traders will usually be the first people to start buying and selling the tokens on public exchanges.

The first ICO took place in 2013 when Seattle's J.R. Willett raised $500,000 in bitcoin for Mastercoin (now branded as Omni), which was a protocol layer that operated on top of bitcoin rather than an entirely new alternative coin. Willett offered 100 Mastercoins for each bitcoin raised – when one bitcoin was worth about $100.

Since the ICO, Omni's market cap has grown dramatically to $50 million, and the price of each Omni coin has risen from a buck to more than $90 come the start of 2018. Buyers who got into the ICO may have been able to multiply the value of their holdings. It's had its ups and downs like any other cryptocurrency, though.

ICO scams and problems

Unfortunately, it's not all good news. There are countless ICOs happening all the time, and the vast majority of new coins won't get very far. Some are even outright scams or ICO pyramid schemes, where people simply hype up and start selling worthless tokens.

However, there's a lot of money to be made in ICOs, for both traders and new companies offering a new coin. By some estimates, 2017 saw more than $3.5 billion pumped into ICOs. If you want to get involved with an ICO, it's important that you know exactly what you're buying and that you make an informed decision.

So how do you choose an ICO? The best ICO to get involved with is one that you understand, can believe in and genuinely think will succeed. Look for professional coins that have clearly had a lot of work put into them, and avoid "get rich quick" schemes. Here are a few tips:

- Understand what the coin is meant to accomplish. It typically needs to fulfill a function in order to become valuable.

- Look at the team behind it and what kind of experience they have. Avoid anonymous ICOs, and consider whether the team has the experience to successfully develop the coin.

- Look at how much research has been done for the coin. Each new coin should come with a published white paper, which is the name given to a document that explains the technology and functionality of the new coin.

- Look at the long-term plans. These will typically be found on the ICO website and in the white paper. The ICO team should have a clear roadmap for the future that extends months, or years, into the future.

- Look at the ICO terms and conditions. A legitimate ICO should make your rights very clear, like detailing the policies on refunds and coin ownership, for example.

- Look at the coin supply limit. This is the total number of coins that will ever be minted. Consider the number of total coins that will ever exist and how many are being released in the ICO. Make sure the price is an accurate reflection of the coin supply. Note: not all coins will have a supply limit.

How to get involved in an ICO

Currently, the most popular way to buy into an ICO is probably with Ether. This is because the Ethereum network is a very useful and flexible platform for creating new applications. You'll often see coins in ICOs specified as ERC20. This generally means it can run on the Ethereum network and can usually be held in an Ethereum-compatible wallet.

Other ICOs will accept bitcoin and other altcoins for payment, or potentially even fiat currencies. However, for cryptocurrency payment, an ICO will commonly require you to sign up on the website and then send the payment from your wallet to the ICO's wallet.

Depending on the value specified for a single coin in the ICO, you will then own a certain amount of this new altcoin. However, there may be a delay before those newly acquired altcoins are sent to your digital wallet and waiting for them to appear can be stressful.

You may also notice ICOs with multiple buy-in points. In order to create a sense of urgency, many ICOs will offer a coin bonus (like 20%), or a cheaper coin price, for early adopters. This bonus may decrease or the price increase in increments over time or as certain allotments are purchased until the ICO is over. If you've found an ICO that you think will succeed, you might want to buy into it. However, before you do buy in, think about a few things in advance:

- **Check the dates:** ICOs are short with tokens only available for a limited time. There are usually weeks or months of advance notice ahead of an ICO's launch and a clear indication of how long it will run for, so don't be caught unaware.

- **Check the prices:** Consider the price next to the supply limit. To give you some perspective, bitcoin has a relatively low 21 million supply limit, while the Ether supply is unlimited – its inflation is capped instead. If you feel that the supply will be such that demand for the coin will be low initially, then you would want the ICO to start at a low price to encourage demand.

- **Check the wallet requirements:** You might need to download a new wallet to support the coin you're purchasing, or you might be able to hold it in your current wallet. Either way, you don't want the ICO creators to send your coins to a wallet that isn't compatible and have them be lost forever. Wallet requirements should be clearly identified on the website.

- **Consult the community:** The Internet is never short of opinions, and that's especially true of the cryptocurrency community. With such technically and financially complex interactions occurring within coins, it's always good to see what those who might know more than you are saying. Hubs like Reddit and Telegram are never short of debate, so either join one or start your own and see what the pros and cons are.

- **Look for red flags:** These might be signs that an ICO is a scam or that it's just a rubbish coin that won't go far. Over the next couple of pages we will give you some tips on what to look out for.

The popularity of ICOs through the start of 2018 has been so great that websites have crashed under the load of traders trying to get in on an ICO's opening day. There is little you can do about this, outside of trying to maximize your Internet speeds at the time by not trying to simultaneously watch Netflix on another screen (or likeminded bandwidth-consuming activity). Just keep refreshing and hope for the best, and make sure that all the sign-up legwork is well and truly done before the ICO goes live.

How to spot an ICO scam

The number one rule used to be that if it seems too good to be true, it probably is. But that rule doesn't always apply to ICOs. The most popular cryptocurrencies have years of development behind them, and today's legitimate and successful ICOs might be aiming to reach maturity years later, with exceptionally ambitious goals. It makes picking a scam from a genuine creator tough, and up to 46% of ICOs will fail in their first year, taking your money with it.

Let's look at a case study!

Consider two real coins that sounded too good to be true. One is legitimate and the other is a scam. One is IOTA, and the other is PlexCoin.

IOTA doesn't use a blockchain. Instead, it uses a directed acyclic graph (DAG) network of its own design called a Tangle. A DAG behaves differently from a blockchain in that the blocks don't necessary chain to each other in a linear fashion, but more like leaves in a tree, all leading back to the original genesis unit (read: trunk).

Through Tangle, IOTA's developers promise to create a cryptocurrency network with zero transaction fees, infinite scalability for an endless number of users to get instant data transfer and potential compatibility with almost any device imaginable. It's an ambitious project that uses buzzwords to make promises that sound too good to be true.

However, it's also a legitimate, transparent and viable open-source project, and this roadmap and all the details were available in the white paper. The value of IOTA tokens has multiplied since the ICO, and its ICO traders are very happy with their decision to buy.

PlexCoin is on the other end of the spectrum. It skipped over all the technical details and instead offered some fairly basic features, most of which already exist. All the details were vague, except its promise of a 1,354% return in the first month. This alone makes it almost certain that it's an ICO scam. No legitimate ICO will ever guarantee a return.

Its creators are also anonymous, and there are no details on the team behind it. But if there were, they might show that "PlexCorp" was created by a Canadian businessman named Dominic Lacroix who has previously been charged with six counts of fraud. Despite that, it managed to raise more than $15 million from unsuspecting traders afraid of missing out on the next big thing.

You can still find its website, although you probably won't be able to make a purchase even if you wanted to. Its accounts have been frozen by the US Security and Exchange Commission (SEC). In addition, its creator woulld have been charged with illegally profiting from defrauding customers.

Scam ICO red flags

Look for signs of a scam and indications that it might not be a very successful purchase. These are dead giveaways:

- Empty repositories for open-source projects. This is when they claim to be open source, but have no published documentation.

- No communication channels. Trust is crucial for an ICO, and a legitimate one should be ready to earn it by being easy to contact.

- An unknown or underskilled team. A management team that doesn't provide their real-world identities or a group that doesn't have any crypto-related experience among them probably won't be able to create a successful coin.

Garbage ICO red flags

It's not just a scam you have to be wary of. You also need to be able to pick an ICO that has an actual future and potential to rise in value. Does it have a use case that will create demand? Here are typical traits of garbage ICOs.

- **Serves no purpose:** Becoming valuable is not a purpose. A coin needs to be able to do something in order to become valuable. For example, one goal might be to be the native token of a revolutionary new system that offers real value to users.

- **Imbalanced premine:** The premine refers to the coins that are reserved for the development team and set aside prior to the ICO. It's meant to cover ongoing costs of development. If too many are hoarded by the inside team, it suggests that they're more interested in getting rich quick than creating a usable system.

- **No clear roadmap:** There should be a clear series of objectives for the developers to achieve following the ICO and estimated dates for completion of each. How do they intend to spend your money?

- **An inexperienced or unknown team:** Creating a successful cryptocurrency isn't easy. Most reputable ICOs will have experienced backers or developers who are willing to put their reputation behind the project and have previous successes under their belt.

- **Legal:** You should also look for ICOs that are committed to working in line with all government regulations where possible. If they aren't, the entire project might later be on thin ice and prone to being shut down by regulators.

ICO laws and regulations

ICOs are regulated differently around the world. They might be off limits to traders from certain countries or might have their own terms and conditions to satisfy regulations. For example, in China all ICOs were banned outright. It's difficult to determine what happens when an ICO breaks the law. It depends on the situation, but in the examples to date, there are generally three potential outcomes:

1. The ICO refunds buyers where applicable and either shuts down or takes action to work with regulations.

2. Where there were clearly activities that were deliberately shady, those behind the ICO have been charged with fraud or similar. The difficulties around cryptocurrency mean buyers are typically not refunded.

3. The ICO takes the money and disappears without any consequences. This is the Internet after all.

Whenever you buy into an ICO, remember that there's always a decent chance of losing all your money.

With some due diligence, you can minimize the chances of this. And such is the potential rise in value of an ICO if it succeeds, that you don't need to use a lot of money to reap substantial rewards years later.

How to find an ICO

Simply search for upcoming ICOs and you'll find hundreds of them. An increasing number of aggregators are appearing, which list all ICOs, their key dates and link straight to important documentation like white papers. Just remember that most of them probably won't go too far. Look for the ones that offer more use, more practicality and show every sign of being set up for success.

In many cases, you'll also notice that they only accept certain currencies. The most commonly accepted are Ether and bitcoin, so you might need to buy one of those first and then trade it for the ICO coin. By now, you will have a good idea of that process after having read the earlier chapters in this book.

We mentioned earlier that you can buy ICOs with fiat currency. The majority of ICOs won't accept fiat currency buy-ins, although some will. By avoiding direct fiat currency token sales, ICOs can reduce their regulatory burden and easily offer their coins to a worldwide audience. It all depends on the ICO, where it is based and from where it is trying to receive the money.

A second case study

Let's take a look at a lesser known altcoin called Augur. As the name suggests, Augur is a fortune-telling platform. It's a decentralized platform built on the Ethereum blockchain to crowdsource predictions. It allows its users to make predictions. They get rewarded for accurate predictions and lose out on inaccurate ones. For example, users might wager 50 cents (in crypto money) on a sports match that has a 50/50 chance. If they're correct, they get back a dollar, and if they're wrong, they lose the 50 cents.

Collectively, all these predictions have come together with an unusually high rate of accuracy, often with a higher success rate than any individual expert. The Augur ICO ran from August 17, 2015, to October 1, 2015, during which it sold 8.8 million tokens at less than a dollar each (out of a pool of 11 million) to raise $5.1 million.

At the start of 2018, each of those tokens was worth about $85.

VII. WHAT IS AN ALTCOIN?

We've mentioned the term altcoin a number of times in this book already, but what does this commonly used term actually mean? It's a quite literal term. At first there was just bitcoin, but now there are many alternative coins – the altcoins. Come the start of 2018, there were over 1500 altcoins trading on the open market, and hundreds more in various stages of their ICO offerings.

Altcoins began life as little more than bitcoin copies attempting to mimic bitcoin's successful run, but they quickly became much more than their name suggests. While many are still struggling to break the mold set by bitcoin and make a name for themselves, some are doing truly amazing things with the technology.

From rethinking the entire concept of what the blockchain could and should be used for (Ethereum) to building a purely anonymous and secure network for peer-to-peer transactions (Monero), more and more altcoins are addressing the shortcomings of bitcoin every day. They are innovating on its basic driving technology to go on and become market leaders themselves.

Altcoins are the new kid on the block and they are as unpredictable as they are exciting. With the biggest altcoins vying to take the top spot from bitcoin, they are all attempting to carve their own niches, with goals nothing short of reimagining the way we do business, how we send and receive money and how we transfer assets like properties and cars.

The majority of these coins will struggle to ever gain widespread recognition in the general public. Bitcoin still owns between 35% and 40% of the total market. The top 10 cryptocurrencies control 80%. And the top 30 control 90%. It leaves the best part of 1500 other altcoins to fight over the remaining 10%.

At the end of this guide, we will walk you through the most popular cryptocurrencies, but we also have a full list of the available coins on the finder.com website. Note that every cryptocurrency has a shorter code that represents it, making it easier to show them on live price websites with hundres of listed coins. For example, bitcoin is represented by BTC, Ripple is XRP, and so forth.

It is important to know the shorthand code for the altcoin you are interested in if you want to accurately monitor its price and keep abreast of the latest news.

What's the difference between a coin and a token?

Spend even just a little bit of time researching the cryptocurrency market and you will see both the term "coin" (short for altcoin) and "token" used. At first, they appear almost interchangeable, but there is a difference between the two.

A coin is a cryptocurrency that functions on its own blockchain. It may have begun as a fork of bitcoin (see the next chapter for more on that), but it now exists as its own independent coin, tracking its transactions on its own blockchain ecosystem. A token, on the other hand, piggybacks on an existing blockchain. If you imagine a particular cryptocurrency with its own blockchain, let's say Ethereum, as a mobile phone, then a token is like an app working on that phone.

At a trading level, both token and coins function in the same way. However, as a token is inherently linked to the platform it operates on, not only can its price be impacted by value changes elsewhere in the ecosystem, but you will need to double-down on your research to make sure that the token is doing something significantly different from the parent cryptocurrency and other tokens that use it.

Some examples of coins include bitcoin, Ether, Ripple, Bitcoin Cash, Cardano, Litecoin, NEO, Stellar, IOTA and NEM. Some examples of tokens include EOS, TRON, Tether, VeChain, ICON, Populous, OmiseGo, Binance Coin, Status and Aeternity.

VIII. FORKS IN THE BLOCKCHAIN

Bitcoin frequently forks, as do many other cryptocurrencies. Forks are what happen when a cryptocurrency's software gets changed or upgraded. Because a blockchain is decentralized, running across thousands of different users' computers at a time, the process of making changes is difficult.

Developers can't simply force software changes onto the blockchain in the way Microsoft might force an update into Windows. Instead, they have to make changes available and then convince all users to install them and switch over to the new version. There are two types of fork to consider:

Hard fork: This occurs when the new blockchain and software are incompatible with the old one. In this case, an entirely new coin is created.

Soft fork: The new software or blockchain features are compatible with the old one and there is no new coin created.

At the time of a hard fork, the entire blockchain is cloned. This duplicates its entire transaction history and all the coins on it. But this clone has different DNA. For example, the newly cloned species might have a larger block size or better encryption than the previous one. It's like an entirely new species of coin that is released into the wild.

A fork is considered successful if all the users install the updates and move over to the modified new version of the blockchain. The old blockchain goes extinct and the new one smoothly takes its place. However, a fork can fail. This occurs when only a few or no users upgrade. Without enough users, the new cryptocurrency quickly goes extinct and the new coin becomes unusable and worthless.

But what happens if its half and half? This results in a contentious or experimental fork. Some users will upgrade, but some will stick to the old fork. Others will even start using both. Now there are two species of coin, both of which are alive and well.

Anyone can fork a cryptocurrency whenever they want, so they're happening all the time. Some forks are hobby projects, some are genuine attempts to improve a popular coin and some are outright scams. For example, the "Bitcoin Platinum" fork was attracting some attention until it was revealed to be a hobby scam by a South Korean teenager. His aim was to create uncertainty in the market while he shorted bitcoin.

Some altcoins started life as contentious or experimental forks:

- **Bitcoin Cash (BCH):** Bitcoin Cash forked away from bitcoin on August 1, 2017, in order to offer a larger 8MB block size which would result in cheaper and faster transactions. It was valued at around US$1,400 at the start of 2018.

- **Bitcoin Gold (BTG):** Bitcoin Gold forked away from bitcoin on October 25, 2017, changing the mining system. It aimed to decentralize mining and take it out of the hands of those with powerful ASIC machines so that people could mine it with GPUs (home computers).

- **Dash (DASH):** A relatively early bitcoin fork from 2014, it was designed to enable quicker and cheaper transactions. It has been forked a number of times and spawned other new coins.

Do forks mean free money?

In many cases, yes. Because they create a snapshot of the existing network, the new ecosystem will also replicate the coins being held by users. The new coin delivery to existing users is sometimes known as an airdrop.

In most cases, the new coin will be worthless, but in other instances, it will go on to become a valuable currency in its own right. To get your free money, you will typically need to have the to-be-forked coin held in a wallet of your own rather than on an exchange (otherwise the exchange will get the coins). You will also need to check that your chosen wallet supports the new coin.

Although this may sound fantastic, in truth, money of any kind is only worth the value we ascribe to it. In most cases, a fork will just end up creating worthless or near-worthless money. If a fork doesn't get enough users to process transactions or to start trading it, the new currency will usually just fizzle out of existence. And if exchanges and wallets refuse to support it, the coin is also likely to be worthless.

In order to actually achieve value, fork developers generally need to lay some groundwork, build a reputation and let various services look at the source code beforehand in order to make sure they can work with it.

If you're entitled to free coins from a fork, you generally don't need to do anything to actually claim it. It will automatically be created in your wallet as the founding blockchain is cloned. Even if you can't actually claim or use it right away, it's still going to be waiting for you. There's no expiration date. As long as you've prepared appropriately, you'll be able to access it whenever you're ready.

When will a fork happen?

Forks happen too frequently to prepare for all of them, but fortunately you don't need to. In order to be successful, a fork depends on having a decent proportion of users come aboard right away. This means there's usually a good amount of publicity around legitimate forks, and their due dates are typically specified well in advance.

Bitcoin forks are timed by block height. This refers to the specific block at which the fork will occur. The further away it is, the more difficult it is to predict when exactly it's going to happen. As the date gets closer, it becomes possible to predict it down to the day, the hour and eventually the minute.

This is because the block creation rate depends on the amount of mining power being used on the network. When the specified block size is reached, the network will be cloned and adjusted, and the new blockchain will take off.

Any transactions made on the old blockchain after that block size will not be part of the new blockchain. So if you received 10 bitcoin after the specified block height, you won't be getting airdropped coins on the new blockchain.

To ensure you get any free money that might be on the way, consider the following steps:

1. Make sure you've moved your to-be-forked coins into a private wallet or checked whether your exchange has promised to support the new coin by awarding users their airdrop.

2. Check that your chosen wallet can support the coin. Reputable forks should publicly publish their source code well ahead of time. This lets wallet developers make sure they can accommodate it and that it's safe to let in.

3. Decide whether the forked coin is going to be more like an American dollar or more like a Zimbabwean dollar. Exchanges will often pre-sell fork coin futures for people who want to buy a new coin ahead of its release. If you have faith in the new coin, this can be a way to get it for cheap.

The way a pre-sell works varies by exchange. Typically, they'll simply create a new token that can be redeemed for the new coin at a 1:1 rate after the fork. This can also be a good way of gauging community interest in the new coin. Will there be a big pick-up by the community upon its availability?

What to do during and after a fork

If an exchange or wallet is bringing in a newly forked token, it will typically freeze transactions in the lead-up to, and after, onboarding the new coin. As a general rule, you'll want to avoid making transactions during a major fork. Also consider the following:

- Don't perform any transactions with a newly forked currency until it's known to be safe and functional.

- Be extremely cautious when downloading a brand new wallet to accommodate a forked coin. As a rule of thumb, you don't want to trust a wallet or forked coin that's not open source and hasn't been thoroughly assessed by other users.

What do bitcoin forks mean for its prices?

User communities will sometimes oppose forks on the grounds that duplicating their currency will inevitably devalue it. There's a concern it provides unwanted competition and that all the disruption will hurt prices. This is typically not borne out in reality, though.

In most cases, a successful fork ends up being great news for traders. News of an upcoming fork and coin airdrop often causes a buying spree, which pushes prices upwards.

If public opinion is largely against the new forked coin, users will often immediately use it to buy more of the old coin. This can push prices up even further. Plus, if the coin goes on to become valuable in its own right, users who held onto it just got free money.

IX. WHAT IS A CRYPTOCURRENCY WALLET?

If you're interested in using cryptocurrencies like bitcoin or Ether, whether you want to make purchases with the coins, trade them or hold them, you're going to need a wallet.

While these digital software wallets might behave like regular wallets at first glance, there is a lot to learn about them, including how they work, the different types and, most importantly, how to keep them safe.

Cryptocurrency wallets, (or wallets for short), are pieces of software that give you access to any cryptocurrency that you own. But the name is a bit of a misnomer since your coins are not actually stored in your wallet. The coins do not technically exist anywhere as they do not have any physical form (hence the name digital currency).

What your wallet can do is connect to and analyze the blockchain, which allows you to transfer and receive money to and from other users of that blockchain and check out your coin balance. Some wallets have other features, such as checking live exchange rates to your fiat currency of choice or maintaining various coin balances from different blockchains, but we'll cover these in later sections.

Since the blockchain contains all the transactions that have been made since the initialization of the cryptocurrency, your wallet holds the proof of ownership of a particular transaction. Through all the transactions on the blockchain, a wallet can figure out and verify how many coins you have.

For example, Alice sends Bob 0.001 bitcoin (BTC). Once verified and added to the blockchain, the transaction can then be used by Alice's wallet to show a reduction of 0.001 BTC from her balance and by Bob's wallet to show an addition of 0.001 BTC. All wallets have a record of this transaction. All transactions on the blockchain are public, so all users on the blockchain can confirm that the bitcoin did indeed change hands.

How do coin transactions work?

Inside every wallet, the two most important pieces of data are the public key and the private key. This is how most of today's secure transactions work. For example, when you enter "https://" into your browser to see products on a merchant website, you are using a secure transaction. It makes sense that cryptocurrencies have adopted this method.

The public and private keys come together when it's time to transfer coins from one user to the other. In the example above, Bob gives Alice his public key, which Alice uses with her wallet to send the money. Meanwhile, on the blockchain, Bob's private key is used to match the public key of the recipient of these bitcoins and, once they match, the transaction is added onto a block and appended to the blockchain. With that transaction validated, the money appears in Bob's wallet.

This is why keeping your wallet secure and taking steps to ensure that your private key is secure is of utmost importance. Without it, all your coins will be lost.

The five different types of crypto wallets

As we've just covered, wallets are little more than a way to store two keys, one public address (think of it as the mailing address) and one extremely important private key (think of it as the key that opens the mailbox). Various companies have developed not only software, but different types of real-world wallets to hold these keys, providing different levels of security and ease-of-use.

The five types of crypto wallets can be divided into soft wallets and hard wallets. Soft wallets are downloadable software programs for your PC or phone, while hardware wallets are physical vaults that store cryptocurrency on a specially designed hard drive contained in the device. Soft wallets are typically "hot" while hardware wallets are "cold."

A wallet is hot when it's connected to the Internet. Nothing on the Internet is 100% secure, so funds kept in a hot wallet are always at a slight risk of theft or loss from software bugs. A wallet is cold when it's safely offline and can't be deliberately or accidentally compromised over the Internet.

Desktop wallet: These are the most common types of wallet and are downloaded and installed on your computer or laptop. They are easy to install and maintain, and most are available for Windows, Linux and Mac, although some are limited to a particular operating system. Most, if not all cryptocurrencies, offer a desktop wallet specifically designed for their coin. While third-party companies operate solutions that allow various coins to be held in one wallet.

Desktop wallets provide a very high level of security since they're accessible only from the machine on which they're installed. The biggest disadvantage is that they also rely on you to keep your computer secure and free of malware. So antivirus and anti-malware software, a strong firewall and a common-sense approach to security are required to keep your coins safe and sound.

Most desktop wallets will provide you with a long string of words upon installation. These words map with your private key and effectively become the password or proof of ownership. As such, it's important to store them somewhere safe in case your computer dies or you need to format the operating system and re-install your desktop wallet.

Online wallets: Online wallets (most often owned by exchanges, but sometimes owned by third-party organizations) run on the cloud and are the easiest to set up and use. Some only require an email address and a password, although the more secure ones require other verification such as a scan of your passport or other ID.

The biggest advantages to online wallets are that they cannot be accidently lost and that they're accessible from any computer or mobile device with an Internet connection. Businesses keeping online wallets for users also often have servers that are far more secure than the average user's computer.

However, being online is unfortunately also their biggest disadvantage. Because some businesses maintain the wallets of thousands of users, they are the biggest targets for hackers. After all, why would a hacker attack your wallet when it can attack thousands at once? Additionally, some online wallets will take a percentage (or flat) fee for every transaction you carry out, which could quickly eat into your balance (or profits, if you're a trader) unless you're careful.

Smartphone wallets: These are similar to desktop wallets, but they run as an app on your phone. They enjoy most of the same advantages and disadvantages of regular, desktop wallets. Smartphone wallets are often simpler and easier to use compared to their desktop counterparts and include the ability to scan other wallet addresses for faster transactions.

You will need to be extra careful about losing your smartphone, though, because anyone who has access to your device might also have access to your funds.

Hardware wallets: Also very similar to desktop wallets, hardware wallets add another layer of security by keeping the private key on a small portable hard drive. These wallets work a lot like a USB stick and are specifically tailored to secure cryptocurrency. Apart from added security, hardware wallets allow the user to plug the USB stick into any computer, log in, make a transaction and unplug.

The biggest disadvantage here is that if you lose the USB stick, you lose your private key, so you'll need to be extra careful about keeping the stick safe. That said, depending on the model you purchase, they'll typically require you to enter a PIN in order to access it, and have some backup options in the event of device loss.

Ledger Nano S, KeepKey and TREZOR are all extremely popular hardware wallets. Their prices range from roughly $50 to $100, depending on the device.

Paper wallets: Paper wallets take the concept of entirely offline keys used for hardware wallets to the next logical step. You simply print out your public and private keys and use that printout as your wallet. That we are allowed to keep paper wallets is a testament to the power of the blockchain transaction.

As secure as they are, paper wallets are also the most complex wallets to use since they require both the paper and a desktop (or software) wallet to work. They should only be used by the most advanced users who want the highest level of security possible.

To transfer money to a paper wallet, you use a software wallet (any of the above we mentioned) to send money to the public key printed on the sheet of paper. Most often, this is printed as a QR code for easy scanning. To transfer money from the paper wallet to someone else, you would first need to transfer money to a software wallet (by manually entering the private key into the software), and then transfer money from the software wallet to the recipient as usual.

Sending and receiving coins with your wallet

Wallets not only allow you to check your available balance, they also allow you to send and receive cryptocurrency. Wallets vary from one to another in how they handle the sending and receiving of currency, but the general process remains the same.

Sending: First, you will need a wallet address (the recipient's public key). This could be an individual, an exchange, a company, an ICO or, in the future, a retail outlet. These addresses are given in one of three ways:

- A long alphanumeric string (numbers and letters)

- A QR code (for smartphone wallets)

- A URL-like web link (clickable, opens your wallet automatically)

Once the address is entered into the wallet, you will be asked to enter an amount of cryptocurrency to send. Once you've entered the amount, click your wallet's version of a send button. The recipient will immediately be notified of the transaction.

Receiving: Receiving coins is even easier than sending them. However, wallets vary greatly in the way this is done. Some will provide you with a fixed public address while some will give you a new address for every transaction. Most will provide a combination of the two.

Whichever system your wallet uses, you will have to provide a public key in one of the formats listed in the previous section to the sender along with how much money you're asking for. Once sent, you should receive a notification of the transaction. Depending on the blockchain in use, the transaction might take some time to be verified because in most cases a miner needs to confirm the request and add the transaction to the blockchain. This might be anywhere between a few seconds to ten minutes (or longer) depending on the cryptocurrency being used.

Keeping your wallet secure

Your wallet might not contain your actual coins, but it's the gateway to those funds. Coins are sent to a combination of your public and private keys, and if that combination is lost (by, say, accidentally uninstalling your desktop wallet), you will never be able to match those transactions to yourself, and all your digital currency will be lost.

So how do you make sure you keep your coins? By keeping your wallets secure and employing standard best practices. Wallets are built to be secure. They are almost completely unhackable and the weakest link is most often the user. So make sure to follow standard security best practices when using a desktop wallet on a computer or when accessing an online/smartphone wallet. Here are some additional tips:

Research before you choose. Don't just choose the first bitcoin wallet you come across. Thoroughly research the security features and development team behind a range of wallets before making your final decision.

Enable 2-factor authentication. This is a simple security feature available on an increasing number of wallets. It's easy to use and provides an extra layer of protection for your wallet.

Pick your password carefully. Don't be lazy when choosing a password. Make sure all usernames, PINs and passwords related to your crypto wallet are strong.

Consider a multisignature wallet. Multisig wallets require more than one private key to authorize a transaction, which means another user or users will need to sign each transaction before it can be sent. Though this means it'll take a little longer to send funds, you may find that the extra peace of mind is well worth the minor hassle.

Update your antivirus protection. Your PC, laptop, smartphone or tablet should have the latest antivirus and anti-malware software installed. Set up a secure firewall on your computer and never install software from companies you don't know.

Update your wallet software. Regularly update your wallet software to always have the latest security upgrades and protections.

Make a backup. Have a wallet backup stored in a safe place so you can recover your crypto funds if something goes wrong — like if you lose your smartphone.

Check the address. When sending or receiving funds, use the correct wallet address. Similarly, if using an online wallet, make sure it is secure by checking that its URL starts with "https://"

Don't use public Wi-Fi. Never access your wallet over a public Wi-Fi network.

Split your holdings. Consider splitting your crypto coins up between online and offline storage. For example, keep a small portion of your funds in online storage for quick and convenient access, and store the bulk of your holdings offline for extra security.

Private key protection. Never share your private key with anyone. Check whether the wallet you choose allows you to keep full control of your private keys, or if you'll have to surrender ownership to a third party such as an exchange.

If you're using a desktop, smartphone or online wallet and follow these best practices, your coins should stay safe. It is wise to periodically change your password information just to be extra safe.

What you need to know about backups

Most people nowadays backup their vacation photos, their texts, their documents and even their game saves. Keeping a backup of your wallet is no different. Most desktop wallets will let you define a backup folder upon installation. Every time you are done making a transaction, you should always save a copy of the backup folder onto a USB stick in case something happens to your computer. This will let you recover your wallet since it will contain your private key.

Backups should always be done on an offline medium. Keeping your wallet's backup on the cloud could lead to disaster if that backup service provider is hacked. Additionally, if your wallet provides you with a key (as discussed in an earlier section) you should keep a copy (or two or three copies) of that key just in case.

Finally, make sure to keep a copy of your usernames and passwords in a secure location just in case you only access your wallet occasionally (after all, you should be using a password so strong you can barely remember it even with regular use).

Why you need 2FA

Some wallets require only a username and password to access them. Other wallets have two-factor authentication or require a PIN-code generator to access them. The more security layers a wallet provides the better. It might make it a hassle to access and transfer funds quickly, but your money is better safe than sorry.

Used by the most secure and trustworthy wallets, two-factor authentication requires a regular username and password combination and another authentication method. This is often a PIN code that is sent to your smartphone as an SMS and is different every time you log in. This means that an attacker needs to know your username and password, and also has to be in possession of your phone.

Some wallets also require the use of a secondary app installed on your smartphone that generates these PIN codes for you, again adding another layer of security.

What wallet should you use?

Your next course of action depends on where you are on the cryptocurrency adventure. If you have yet to decide on a cryptocurrency to buy, check out some of the guides on the finder website for the latest price guides. If you've already decided on a favorite coin, there are a few things to consider before you choose a wallet.

- **Your personality.** This factor comes down to personal preference. For example, if security is your number-one priority, compare hardware wallets. But if your want to quickly and conveniently access your coins, a mobile or web wallet may be your preferred choice.

- **Ease of use.** Sending, receiving and storing crypto can be complicated and confusing, particularly for beginners. So, any wallet you choose should suit your tech knowledge and level of crypto experience. So while crypto novices might focus on finding a wallet that's simple to set up and use, experienced holders seek advanced features, like an in-wallet exchange and multisignature transactions.

- **Security features.** Find out what security features the wallet includes, such as 2-factor authentication and multisig functionality. Will your private key be stored online or offline? Has the wallet ever suffered any security breaches?

- **Range of features.** Check what other features the wallet includes, like the ability to exchange between currencies within your wallet or providing easy access to live fiat exchange rates or other market information.

- **Supported cryptocurrencies.** Are you looking for a wallet that stores one crypto, like bitcoin, or are you in the market for a multi-currency wallet? Make sure the wallet you choose is compatible with the cryptocurrencies you need to store, and remember that some coins and tokens can only be held in an official wallet.

- **The team behind the wallet.** See what you can find out about the people behind the wallet. How long have they been in business? What qualifications do they have? Are they continually working to upgrade and improve the wallet?

- **Cost.** While most crypto wallets are free, choosing a hardware wallet means you'll have to part with some cash. Consider the upfront price and shipping costs when making your decision. Some wallets also charge a fee for every transaction you make, so read the fine print to see what you'll pay.

- **Reputation.** What level of community trust does the wallet have? Check out independent online reviews to gauge how other users rate the wallet and whether they would recommend it.

On the finder website, we have multiple reviews and a comparison tool that can help.

If you want to hold onto your crypto, there's typically not much you need to do once the funds are in your wallet. You can log into your wallet whenever you want to check your balances. You can earn interest on some currencies by staking your holdings, though there may be specific instructions in your wallet to do this. If you keep it safe, your wallet will become your next best friend.

X. WHAT IS AN EXCHANGE?

Exchanges are where you buy and sell cryptocurrencies, so they're an integral part of the market. But no two are alike, and it's worth doing your research before picking one. Online exchanges are much like their brick-and-mortar counterparts. They let you convert one currency to another. In the case of cryptocurrencies, this might be converting fiat currency (USD, AUD, EURO, etc.) to a cryptocurrency or trading one cryptocurrency for another.

To use an exchange, you usually need to do the following:

1. **Create an account:** In many cases, you'll also need to verify your identity by providing a copy of your driver's license or other proof. It can take some time, depending on demand, to get verified.

2. **Deposit funds into your account:** You usually need to have funds in your account to start trading. Since getting a currency into your account uses traditional fiat transacted by a bank, it can take 24-hours or more to be processed.

3. **Withdraw your funds when ready:** For security reasons, it's standard practice to withdraw and hold funds yourself over keeping them in your exchange account.

How do I hold funds outside of an exchange?

As detailed in the previous chapter, cryptocurrencies are held in digital wallets. These can usually be downloaded and installed to your phone or PC in just a few minutes. But for more secure long-term storage, standard practice is to hold funds safely offline in a hardware wallet or another type of offline physical storage.

When your cryptocurrency is held in your account on an exchange, it means it's being held in an online wallet owned by that exchange. Sometimes you will be able to hold your funds there indefinitely, while other cryptocurrency trading might require you to have your own wallet before starting.

Remember that for all intents and purposes, cryptocurrency being held on an exchange is in the possession of the exchange, not you. For example, if you own a coin that pays dividends, those will be paid to the exchange. Whether the exchange will then pass those dividends on to you depends on the exchange.

You don't necessarily need a wallet to start trading, but once you know which coins you want to buy, it's usually a good idea to start looking for a wallet to accommodate them.

What is the difference between exchanges?

There's no shortage of exchanges for you to use, and you can compare them using the handy tool on the finder website. Most people will use more than one exchange, using the strengths of each as befits the cryptocurrency they wish to trade in or the fiat currency they intend to use. Here are a couple of the main differences you're likely to see:

- **The coins they carry:** Some exchanges only sell bitcoin, while others might let you trade dozens of different cryptocurrencies. Sometimes a coin will only be available on one or two exchanges.

- **Whether they support fiat currency:** Some of the largest exchanges only deal with cryptocurrencies and don't let you deposit or withdraw fiat currencies. Some exchanges only let your transfer money in a certain fiat currency or from banks in a particular country. Some accept credit cards or even PayPal, too. (Note: If you're looking for a good credit card to use for trading, the comparison tool on the finder website is unmatched!)

- **The fees the exchanges charge:** The two main types of fees are those charged for trading and for making deposits or withdrawals from your account. The option that offers the best value for your money will depend on your specific plans. For example, you might find different withdrawal fees for different coins or trading fees that vary by volume.

- **What type of exchange it is:** There are three main types of exchanges, and each is quite different. Knowing the different types can make it easier to compare exchanges at a glance and rule out the ones you're not interested in.

The three different types of exchanges

While each exchange has its own method of doing things, they generally fall into one of three different categories:

Brokers

Best for: Crypto novices, those looking for a quick and easy way to buy cryptocurrency. *The downsides:* Costs more than the other options and brokes may not offer as wide a selection of cryptocurrencies.

Cryptocurrency brokers often offer the simplest and most convenient way to buy a coin or token. Buying bitcoin or any altcoin from a broker is essentially like purchasing from a cryptocurrency shop — the broker buys digital coins or tokens at wholesale rates, adds their own margin on top and then sells the currency on to you. Brokers offer a quick and straightforward entry into the world of cryptocurrency. Their platforms are designed to be easy to use and you can pay for your crypto purchase with your everyday fiat currency, often even by using a credit or debit card.

The main downside of using a broker is the cost, as you'll not only need to buy your crypto at a price above the market rate but also pay transaction fees. Examples of some well-known cryptocurrency brokers include Coinbase and CoinSpot.

Markets

Best for: Buying and selling a wide range of currencies; lower fees.
The downsides: Intimidating for new users and it may not be possible to directly exchange the currencies you want.

Cryptocurrency trading platforms are the most widely used platforms for buying and selling digital currency. They connect crypto buyers with crypto sellers and take a fee for facilitating each transaction. You can use these platforms to exchange cryptos at the current market rate or at a specified limit, while some sites also offer advanced features like stop-loss orders. Crypto trading platforms tend to provide access to a more diverse range of currencies than brokers, and often feature charting tools to help you plan your trades. These platforms tend to offer lower fees and better exchange rates than brokers.

However, it's not possible to directly exchange one crypto for any digital currency you want — you're limited to the trading pairs supported by your chosen platform. Bitcoin and Ether are the most commonly traded currencies and feature in pairs alongside a wide range of altcoins. Crypto trading platforms can also be intimidating and confusing for new users.

Examples of high volume cryptocurrency trading platforms include Binance and Bittrex.

Direct P2P

Best for: Anonymity, giving you more control over how you trade.
The downsides: Prices usually higher than market rates; a certain level of risk involved.

These platforms allow direct peer-to-peer trading between people all around the world. The exchange acts as the middleman, with the seller able to set their own price and accepted payment methods.

The main advantage of peer-to-peer exchanges is that they let you anonymously and quickly buy or sell coins with almost any kind of trade or payment method you want.

The downside is that you'll often pay above market prices, and it can also be riskier than other options. To help offset the risks, some platforms have built-in escrow features and reputation systems to identify reliable and legitimate buyers and sellers.

Examples of peer-to-peer exchanges include LocalBitcoins and Paxful.

Centralized vs. Decentralized Exchanges

If you're researching P2P exchanges, you'll also come across the concept of decentralized crypto exchanges. Many (but not all) peer-to-peer exchanges can also be decentralized in their design. Decentralized exchanges (DEXs) are hosted on a network of distributed nodes and allow you to trade cryptocurrency directly with other users.

The absence of centralization means there's no single point of failure for hackers to target, and server downtime is no longer an issue. Plus, because trades are executed using smart contracts, you can trade straight from your wallet. This ensures that you don't have to transfer any of your coins and tokens onto an exchange, allowing you to retain control of your cryptocurrency at all times.

Understanding exchange fees

There are three main types of fees that might be incurred on an exchange.

- **Deposit fee:** This is the fee for depositing funds into your account. These are usually not charged by the exchange itself, but rather by your bank, credit card, money transfer or wallet provider as the cost of a transfer. If you'll be converting currencies, such as from USD to EUR, this will also usually cost more.

- **Trading fee:** This is the fee for making a trade and is usually charged as a percentage of the total trade volume. You'll often get charged around 3% commission by brokers (if they are used) or 0.1-0.5% in fees per trade on other exchanges. Trading fees can vary depending on the difficulty required in confirming a transaction at the time.

- **Withdrawal fee:** This is the fee for withdrawing funds from the exchange to your own wallet or bank account. It usually depends on the type of currency being withdrawn and is charged as a flat amount to help cover the exchange's transfer costs for sending you the money.

The exchange with the best value for your money will depend on the currencies you're trading, your planned trade volume, how frequently you'll be making withdrawals and the coin prices themselves. For example, you might end up with better value for money at a seemingly expensive exchange that accepts your country's currency simply because it lets you avoid currency conversion costs.

It's also worth considering these fees when looking for possible arbitration opportunities. This occurs when one exchange appears to be selling a cryptocurrency at a significantly lower price than they are being bought on another exchange. This gives you an opportunity to buy on one and sell on another, making a profit on the margin. However, the fees and the time it takes for a transaction to be confirmed can close that margin and leave you at a loss if you are not careful.

How to choose the right exchange

Exchanges come in various shapes and sizes, from those that offer multiple levels of security to those that don't even ask you to create an account. So when you're about to choose an exchange, it's best to look at its features and go from there. Here is a guide on how to interpret those features:

- **Types of trading:** First, consider the type of trades you want to place. There are exchanges available that offer;

    - Fiat-to-crypto trading

    - Crypto-to-crypto trading

    - Both fiat-to-crypto and crypto-to-crypto trading.

  For example, if you want to purchase BTC with USD, you'll need to find a cryptocurrency broker that allows you to buy coins via bank transfer or credit card. Alternatively, if you want to exchange your BTC or ETH holdings for another cryptocurrency, you'll want a platform that offers direct crypto-to-crypto trades.

- **Trading pairs:** Consider which currencies you want to trade, and which platforms list those currencies in one or more trading pairs. There are more than 1,600 digital currencies in existence as of August 2018, so don't expect to find them all listed on any single platform. Major cryptos like BTC, ETH, XRP and others in the top 20 coins by market cap are listed on an extensive range of exchanges, but rarer altcoins may be much harder to find and pair with cryptocurrencies you already own. Also, if you want to buy crypto with one or more fiat currencies, check which deposit currencies the platform accepts.

- **The fees:** Fees vary widely from exchange to exchange and can pile up if you're not careful. To find out how much you'll actually be paying, consider running the numbers on a hypothetical trade before the real thing, with the same payment method, volume, coins and withdrawal method. If an exchange does not publicly post its fees, steer away.

- **Payment methods:** Exchanges accept all sorts of different payment methods, from credit and debit cards to bank transfers, but not all exchanges accept all the various payment options. Also note that some exchanges might accept one payment method for withdrawal of cryptocurrency funds, but not for deposits. Some may also have different time delays between when you make the deposit or withdrawal, and when that money becomes available. Make sure your exchange has deposit and withdrawal options that work for you, and make sure to check the fees associated with different methods.

- **Purchase limits:** Exchanges may have limits on how much or how little you can deposit, buy and withdraw at any one time. These limits will often vary depending on the transaction method as well as on your verification level. For example, someone who's provided notarized proof of identity, address and source of their funds might get unlimited transactions, while someone who's only shown their driver's license might be restricted to $1,000 a week. See whether the limits work for your plans.

- **Security:** A large exchange might be holding hundreds of millions of dollars' worth of cryptocurrency. It's typical for around 99% of it to be held offline at any given time, but a successful hacker can still become a multi-millionaire by getting that remaining 1%. Large exchanges tend to be under almost constant attack, and those without effective digital security don't last long.

You can assume that prominent exchanges have decent electronic security, but you should still read reviews and make sure an exchange is legitimate. It's also worth remembering that an exchange that has been hacked in the past isn't necessarily any less secure today. Instead consider how it responded to the hack and whether all affected users were fairly compensated for any losses. Some good questions to ask include:

1. Is 2-factor authentication supported?

2. Are customer funds stored in online or offline wallets?

3. Do I control my private key or does the exchange?

4. If it's the latter, where and how is my private key stored?

5. What level of verification is required to open an account?

6. Is there 24/7 security monitoring?

7. Will you receive email and SMS alerts regarding account activity?

8. Does the exchange use email encryption?

9. Does the exchange provide proof of reserve?

- **Available coins:** Naturally, you'll also want to make sure your preferred coins are available. There's not much point in signing up for an exchange that doesn't have what you want.

- **User friendliness and trader tools:** If you're a cryptocurrency novice, getting started buying and selling coins and tokens can be complicated and confusing. On the other hand, experienced traders may want a platform with special features like advanced charting and order types, and the option to trade on margin. If you're a crypto trading beginner, look for a platform with a simple and straightforward user interface that's easy to understand from the beginning.

- **Ease of access:** How can you access your trading account? For example, many platforms offer web browser-based trading only, but some also offer mobile and even desktop trading apps. If trading on the go is important to you, it's worth reading up on how user friendly the platform's mobile app is.

- **Loyalty programs and discounts:** Is there any way you can reduce trading fees? For example, are you entitled to fee discounts simply because you hold an exchange's native currency or use those tokens to pay transaction fees? Is there a tiered fee structure that rewards high-volume traders with reduced fees? Some crypto exchange loyalty programs even offer additional benefits, such as access to exclusive events and even a share of the platform's trading fee revenue.

- **Exchange rates:** There is no such thing as an official bitcoin price — it's determined by whatever people are willing to pay. Compare exchange rates across a handful of different crypto exchanges and you might be surprised to find just how much they can differ from one platform to the next. The variation can be as much as 10% in some cases, which can make a big difference to the success of a trade.

- **Liquidity:** The level of liquidity on an exchange affects the ease and speed with which you can complete trades. If there's a high level of liquidity — if the exchange has a high trading volume — then trades should be completed quickly and easily. For example, one of the biggest benefits of trading on larger crypto exchanges is that they get enough orders to match buyers and sellers without any difficulty. However, low liquidity can lead to substantial price fluctuations.

You can check crypto exchange trading volumes on sites like CoinMarketCap.

- **Payment method:** Can you deposit funds into your account via bank transfer, credit card or PayPal? The more payment options an exchange has, the more convenient it will be to use. Make sure your exchange has deposit and withdrawal options that work for you, and remember to check the fees associated with different methods.

- **Account verification process:** If privacy is important to you when trading cryptocurrency, there are some platforms that allow you to transact anonymously. Of course, if it's too easy to create an account and start trading, consider whether there's anything to stop a platform from disappearing — hopefully not with your funds — overnight.

  Many other platforms require you to verify your account before allowing you to trade. This step is designed to ensure that the exchange meets its obligations under anti-money laundering and counter-terrorism financing (AML/CTF) regulations. Verification requirements vary between exchanges, but you may need to provide some or all of the following:

    - Your name

    - Your email address and phone number

    - Your address

    - Proof of ID

    - Proof of address]

    - A photo of yourself holding a signed declaration.

  If you need to provide a wide range of personal information, be sure you're dealing with a trusted exchange. It's also a good idea to research how long you can expect the verification process to take. Finally, some exchanges will require you to complete additional verification tasks to unlock full account features and higher transaction limits.

- **Processing times:** How long will it take for your transaction to be completed? How soon are account withdrawals processed? Being forced to miss out on a trading opportunity because your trading funds took too long to arrive into your exchange account can be a frustrating experience.

  Spending day after day waiting for a withdrawal to arrive in your bank account or crypto wallet can also be extremely stressful, so check average processing times before you register.

- **Regulation:** Though authorities around the world are starting to catch up to the rapid growth of crypto exchanges, the industry as a whole is still lightly regulated. How an exchange is regulated depends on where it's based, so do your research to find out whatever information you can about the platform operators. For example, a number of central banks around the world have called for tighter regulations to deter anonymous trading and boost transparency. Although the US has not committed to any new regulations.

  It's also worth noting that due to regulatory requirements, users from certain countries will not be allowed to access some exchanges. As always, check the fine print to find out whether any of these geographical restrictions apply to you.

- **Customer support:** This is a crucial but often overlooked factor when comparing crypto exchanges. If you ever have a problem with an individual transaction or with your account, how will you access a platform's customer support team? You'll need to consider:

    - What are the customer support channels? Do you have avenues through email, phone and live chat?

    - Is there an online support center where you are able to submit a support ticket?

    - Is support available 24/7 or only during specific hours?

    - How quickly does the support team respond to inquiries?

    - If the exchange is based in a country where English isn't the first language, can you find and access English-language support whenever you need it?

    - Does the site's support center feature answers to a range of frequently asked questions, and perhaps instructional guides or videos that explain how to trade?

    - Does the platform have a good reputation for providing prompt and helpful support to users?

- **Reputation:** Does the exchange have a reputation as a secure and reliable platform? Read independent online reviews from other users to find out all about their experiences, both positive and negative, with the platform. Where does it excel and where does it fall short? Would they recommend the exchange to friends and family? Consider how long an exchange has been operating, and if it's fully insured before deciding which platform is right for you.

Exchange payment methods

Crypto exchanges accept all sorts of deposit methods, including:

- Bank transfers

- Credit and debit cards

- Prepaid cards

- PayPal, Neteller, Skrill and other online payment services

- Cash deposits

- Cryptocurrency transfers

However, not all exchanges accept all payment options. To make things more complicated, some exchanges might accept one payment method for withdrawals, but not for deposits. Processing times, fees and limits can all vary depending on the payment method you choose, so read the fine print to learn the ins and outs of each payment option. For example, while credit card deposits might be processed quickly, they usually attract high fees. Meanwhile, bank transfer deposits may not attract any fees, but they can take one to two business days to process.

Should you use an exchange's wallet?

When you buy cryptocurrency on an exchange, those digital coins are typically deposited straight into your exchange wallet. If you want to keep your coins in this wallet, you can. However, think twice about using an exchange for long-term storage. The exchange controls the private key to your wallet, so you effectively don't have total control of your funds. And with exchanges regularly — and sometimes successfully — targeted by hackers, storing bitcoin or any other crypto on an exchange long term is very risky.

A much safer option is to transfer your coins off the exchange and into a secure wallet that lets you control your private key.

How to avoid a crypto exchange scam

While regulators are gradually implementing laws and guidelines to help protect consumers against fraud, there are still plenty of dodgy exchange operators out there. Falling victim to theft is a major concern for crypto buyers. So what can you do to protect yourself against scam crypto exchanges? There are several simple steps you can take:

- **Is the exchange registered with SEC.** Cryptocurrency exchange operators in the US must be registers with the US Securities and Exchange Commission.

- **Is it regulated?** If you're considering using an overseas exchange, find out where exactly it is headquartered and if it has regulatory requirements for digital currency exchanges in that particular country. Does the exchange comply with all of the relevant laws?

- **Do your research.** Don't get sucked in by marketing gimmicks or the promise of a deal that sounds too good to be true. Take your time to research a platform's credentials before opening an account and depositing any funds.

- **Recognize the warning signs.** Recognize the red flags that indicate an exchange is not entirely legit. For example, if there's no information about the company behind the exchange or where it is headquartered, proceed with caution. Similarly, if other users report lengthy withdrawal delays or claim the exchange has engaged in questionable activities, you may be better off steering clear of that platform and seeking another.

- **Check the address.** Whenever you visit an exchange site, check that its address begins with "https" rather than just "http". This means that all communications between your browser and the exchange are secure and encrypted.

- **Only use established exchanges.** Let other people take the risk of trading on new and untested exchanges. You'll sleep a lot better at night if you know you're dealing with an established platform with a good reputation.

For more info on how to stay safe when buying and selling cryptocurrency, check out our guide to bitcoin scams.

XI. STEP-BY-STEP GUIDE FOR CONVERTING FIAT TO A CRYPTOCURRENCY

Now that you have an idea of how you can make transactions within the cryptocurrency world, it's time to look at a real-world example. Exchanges typically have their own specific process for converting fiat currency to cryptocurrency and back, but the general process remains the same.

We'll use a fictitious exchange called LiteExch in this example:

1. Let's say you have $100 to buy Litecoin. You've shopped around and chose LiteExch for your exchange. You like its interface; it carries Litecoin (LTC); it has low fees; and it has a lot of good reviews.

2. After creating an account with LiteExch, you are asked to upload a photo of your passport or driver's license for verification. You go through the process and get verified, which may take several days or even weeks.

3. Upon logging into the account and depending on the payment options available, you may need to deposit that $100 from your bank account to the exchange before you start trading. This can take an extra day or two. However, on some exchanges, you will be able to avoid this step by purchasing with a credit card.

4. Now you're ready to buy some LTC. You find the Buy/Sell section on LiteExch's website and you select "Buy" (because you're buying LTC), choosing your country's fiat as your source currency and LTC for the currency being purchased.

5. Next, you enter $100 into the amount input field, enter your credit card details if this is your payment choice and click the "Next" button.

6. LiteExch now shows you the fees. LiteExch charges 1%, with a $1.50 minimum. Because you're only buying $100 worth of LTC, 1% would come out to $1.00, so you will be charged the minimum of $1.50 instead.

7. The amount of LTC that you will be buying is now shown on your screen. While LTC is trading at $62.50/LTC, you will not be buying 1.600 LTC. Instead, you will be getting 1.576 LTC because the exchange will keep $1.50 of your initial $100.

8. After proceeding with the payment, you now have 1.576 LTC in your exchange wallet, and you go to bed wondering what the next day may bring.

9. When you awake in the morning, you discover that LTC has mooned following a big announcement from the CEO. The value of your LTC has jumped up over 30% and you now have $130 in your wallet on your chosen exchange. Nice trading!

10. Hoping to keep your proceeds safe, you withdraw the funds as a fiat currency back to your bank account, losing 3% in the process in fees. This leaves $126.10 transferred across. Congratulations! You made a profit of $26.10.

XII. SUPPLY, DEMAND AND MARKET VOLATILITY

What defines the value of a cryptocurrency? As mentioned in an earlier chapter, there is a limited supply of any given cryptocurrency in the market. Only a certain amount may have been mined, and some coins have capped amounts that have yet to be reached. It's also important to remember that every cryptocurrency, right down to its smallest fraction, is owned by someone. You can't just go and buy cryptocurrency like you might buy cereal at the local supermarket. If you want to buy cryptocurrency, someone has to sell it. And vice versa, if you want to sell a coin, someone has to be willing to buy it.

This creates a supply and demand situation, and when demand outweighs supply, the value goes up. Sellers can ask more for their cryptocurrency. However, if supply outweighs demand, you will need to offer a competitive price in order to sell, which creates a downward spiral in price until a critical majority of people believe the value is low enough that they want to buy again.

When the price is going up, it's said to be bullish. When it goes down, it's said to be bearish. This rise and fall is a natural correction to overbuying and overselling as it swings between these points. It's only over an extended period of time that we see genuine growth or decline. Predicting this is the role of a technical analysis, which is a good practice for any trader. You can use tools, often provided on exchanges, to examine the overall patterns in a coin's price over time to make smarter bets on when to buy or sell.

What affects the price of a cryptocurrency?

Cryptocurrencies are volatile by nature. They are not as stable as currencies that have had centuries to develop. Bitcoin is the oldest coin on the market, and it has only been around since 2009. The number one thing you'll need to keep in mind when it comes to cryptocurrency trading is that the price is extremely volatile. Where certain trade techniques used in forex might take months to come to fruition, in cryptocurrency trading, it could only take hours or days. While this is beneficial when it comes to making a profit, it could also be your downfall if the price moves the other way.

In September 2017, Litecoin's value fell more than 50% in two weeks. The recovery to its previous value took more than two months. Cryptocurrencies not only take large steps in value both up and down, but they also do so in very short spans of time. The speed at which transactions can occur and at which information can be spread in a landscape where "going viral" and "trending" is a daily occurrence can make it easy for hype or fear, uncertainty and doubt (FUD) to alter the price quickly. This is especially true with a marketplace that extends beyond borders, cultures, languages and governments. The following are some of the things that can affect cryptocurrencies:

- **Regulation:** If a government makes a statement or pushes for a particular regulation that affects cryptocurrencies, you can bet that the price will react to it (sometimes positively, often negatively). When China banned ICOs, the price of Ether fell by 41% in 15 days (from$386.83/ETH to $228.06).

- **Media influence:** Just like government regulation, exposure in the media greatly affects a cryptocurrency's price. Whenever a public figure makes a statement regarding cryptocurrencies or a major retailer starts accepting cryptocurrency as a form of payment, you will see the market respond.

- **Changes to the technology:** When a cryptocurrency's core technology is affected (either via an update or the finding of a flaw), the cryptocurrency's price is also then affected.

- **Whales:** This term is used to describe high rollers. They are big traders with the capital to shift the whole market. Whether it's an individual, or a group of individuals that are colluding together, whales can often stop the natural pattern of the market from unfolding. One of the most influential ways a whale can do this is by setting sell limits. This is where they pre-determine that, once the value of a coin reaches a certain price, they will sell a market-shifting amount of that coin. This can see a coin that appears set to continue upwards growth suddenly get an influx of supply, causing the price to drop.

This is why it's important to not just look at the changes in price when deciding on which cryptocurrency to buy, but the use case for the blockchain technology that the cryptocurrency represents. Examining the team behind a coin, whether what they are trying to achieve has a future, and ensuring that it has runs on the board in terms of achieving that goal, are the best bets to making a wise choice.

What is cryptocurrency burning?

It is possible for the creator of a specific cryptocurrency to burn some of its coins, which makes them unspendable and effectively destroys them. But why would they want to do that? The short answer is that in a supply and demand marketplace, if you burn coins, you reduce the supply and increase the value of the remaining coins. But we have a longer answer, too.

One reason is to pay traders a dividend. Traditionally, a trader who buys shares in a company would receive a monetary dividend on a regular basis. Due to legal complications with this in the cryptocurrency market, some coins use the burn technique as a back-door approaching to awarding a dividend. ICONOMI (ICN) is one such coin. As opposed to paying out a dividend to those who own the coin (effectively, the shareholders), the creators buy back some of the ICN and burn it, reducing supply and increasing the value of the ICN its traders own. Tricky!

A similar strategy is used by some creators who are trying to get a new coin into the market. When initially released, they allow people to buy the coin with bitcoin. They then burn the bitcoin they receive, removing it from the market. This increases the value of bitcoin, and because the new coin is linked to bitcoin, it too rises in value.

Elsewhere, a coin creator might ingrain burning into the way their blockchain technology functions as an alternative to transaction fees. For example, with Ripple (XRP), every time a transaction is made, a small portion of that transaction amount is burned. This reduces supply, increasing demand. As Ripple owns a lot of its own cryptocurrency, it collects an income from this purchase as do other holders.

You'll recall from our earlier chapter on initial coin offerings that these often begin with a set allocation of coins that are sold off to raise funds. Often, if they do not sell all the allotted coins, they'll burn the rest to ensure there isn't an oversupply when they take the new coin to full market trading.

So now that we have established some reasons why a cryptocurrency creator might burn some of its own coins, you may be wondering how they do it. It's actually quite easy. They send the coins to a wallet that is invalid – one that can be verified as an unowned address by anyone in the public who wants to look. This transaction remains lodged in the blockchain, providing what is called proof of burn, and the money can no longer be accessed.

It's kind of sad to think of those poor little coins being sent to their death, isn't it?

XIII. HOW TO TRADE CRYPTOCURRENCY

The value of cryptocurrencies is increasing. In 2017, bitcoin (BTC) alone grew from $1,000 to well over $15,000. The majority of the altcoins also experienced similar rises. With such growth comes an increase in market trading, which in turn helps the currency keep growing. A range of established forex exchanges and brand new platforms are embracing cryptocurrency trading.

Market trading might sound like something reserved for the financial elite, but the growth of cryptocurrency has been accompanied by the growth of online currency exchanges and trading platforms where anyone can take part in market speculation. You just need to know how it works. To help you figure it out, we'll start with an overview of a more traditional trading market.

What is forex market trading?

Foreign exchange (forex) market trading is the buying and selling of currencies between traders. In its simplest form, you're betting on the changing price difference between two different currencies.

You open an account and deposit funds into it. These funds are then used to place buy and sell orders against another currency. You make profits from selling, or closing orders, at a higher price than you bought. There is a beginner's guide to forex trading available on the finder website.

How is cryptocurrency trading different?

Trading cryptocurrencies works exactly the same, but instead of selling and buying fiat currencies, such as euros or US dollars, traders buy and sell cryptocurrencies, such as bitcoin (BTC), Ether (ETH) or Litecoin (LTC).

For example, you might bet on the changing price difference between the US dollar and bitcoin. Or you might bet on the changing values between two different cryptocurrencies by trading currency pairs, such as the BTC/ETH (Ethereum) pair. If you think bitcoin will increase in value, you might "go long" on it. This means betting that it will increase in value relative to the US dollar.

If you think bitcoin will decrease in value, you might "short" it instead. This means betting that it will decrease in value relative to the US dollar.

You're not actually buying the cryptocurrency. Instead, you're just placing an order on the market. Just like forex market trading, cryptocurrency trading works by exchanging one currency into another and back. You will usually exchange a fiat currency into a cryptocurrency and then, at a later date, back into a fiat currency, although there are traders and exchanges that allow cryptocurrency-to-cryptocurrency trading.

So how do you make a profit? When you bet correctly, the funds in your account will increase. There are two types of traders interested in market trading cryptocurrencies:

Long-term trading: Long-term traders buy and hold cryptocurrencies over a long period. They may hold a cryptocurrency for weeks, months or even years. Studying price trends over a long period allows long-term traders to make informed decisions and avoid suffering from short-term dips in value. If you believe the value of a cryptocurrency will grow steadily over a long period and don't want the stress that comes from short-term value dips, then this method might be for you. You're effectively looking at holding cryptocurrency in the hopes that it will grow.

Short-term trading: Short-term trading eschews the stability of long-term trading for the possibility of taking advantage of short-term price swings. It involves the buying and selling of cryptocurrencies over the span of a day or even just a few hours. If you'd rather take advantage of the characteristic volatility of cryptocurrencies by getting in and out of a trade quickly, then this method might be for you. In this example, you're effectively looking at cryptocurrency for trading.

The advantages of trading cryptocurrencies

Trading cryptocurrencies, while similar to trading fiat currencies on forex, comes with its own set of advantages. Below you'll find some of the most notable reasons why you might consider crypto:

- **Cheap fees and fast exchanges:** For each trade, the exchange platform you're using will take a small percentage as commission for the service they're providing. This is inevitable. Where cryptocurrency trades differ from their fiat currency equivalent is in the size of this fee. Because the fees for transferring cryptocurrencies (typically via wallet payments) are cheaper than credit card and bank transfer fees, market-trading fees are cheaper than forex-trading fees.

- **Extreme volatility:** Traders make profits when the price of the currency takes large strides upwards, and cryptocurrencies often experience large price movements. While this increases the risk (large price movements happen downwards as well, of course), you can often make a lot of profit with a relatively small bankroll.

- **Open all week:** You can only trade stocks and commodities during business hours, and you can often only trade forex during standard weekdays. With cryptocurrencies, on the other hand, can be traded 24/7, anytime and anywhere, depending on the exchange.

Things to be careful of when trading cryptocurrency

If you're not careful when it comes to cryptocurrency trading, you could find yourself gambling more than you're trading, and eventually you might lose all your money. Trading is not a game, and just as there is real money to be made, there is real money to be lost. Doing your research and keeping the following concepts in mind when trading could help you avoid the pitfalls of cryptocurrency trading.

Cryptocurrency's volatility: As we've already mentioned, the number one thing you'll need to keep in mind when it comes to cryptocurrency trading is that the price is extremely volatile. Do your research and make sure you are buying on the dip (when a price is heading towards its low point), and then sell on the moon (when the price is rising to its high point.

Patterns sometimes lie: Many market-trading books and guides cover certain chart-reading techniques used by professionals to predict the market. While current trends do sometimes follow past performance, this is never a guaranteed outcome, and unless you limit your exposure, you could end up losing a lot of money acting on a pattern that does not exist.

Limit your exposure: Limiting your exposure comes down to four specific concepts:

- Never risk more money than you are willing to lose. You should consider any money you put into a trade as lost. If you're uncomfortable with this notion, then you're trading more money than you should be. Finding the point where you're comfortable with this concept is key to helping you trade stress-free.

- Consider setting up "take profit" and "stop loss" orders. These limits are offered by many professional trading platforms and can automatically liquidate and "cash out" your position at predefined prices. These are also referred to as buy limits and sell limits.

- Stay away from leverage. Leverage is money that a broker loans you. It's wise to stay away from leverage until you've learned everything you can learn about making trades with your own money. While leverage can help you make greater profits with short cryptocurrency movements, it can also amplify your losses when the trade takes a wrong turn. Always remember, leverage amplifies your winnings and your losses equally. As a beginner, the risks presented when using leverage are typically not worth the possibility of amplified profits.

  Here is a leverage example to better help you understand the concept. You decide to trade $2000 dollars to bitcoin (BTC). Additionally, you leverage another $10,000 from your broker. Now you can buy 1.6 BTC at $7,500/BTC. Later you sell at $8,500/BTC, return the $10,000 and you are left with $3,600, a profit of $1,600 on your initial $2,000. So where the market only grew 13%, the profit grew 80%. Unfortunately, this works the other way around as well. If the price of bitcoin had fallen to $6,500/BTC instead, you would have lost $1,600 plus supplementary costs such as interest, applications cost and fees.

- **Know when to cash out:** What market trading really comes down to is knowing when to close a trade. This is the crux of the operation. Getting into a trade is easy; knowing when to get out is hard, and that is where you should focus most of your learning. This involves two different aspects:

  1. **Closing a trade in profit:** It is important to take your winnings out of a trade. Cryptocurrencies can move down more quickly than they move up and you don't want to be late cashing out of a trade. You also don't want to be too early and miss out on extra profits. There are a lot of techniques to help you make this decision that are beyond the scope of this beginner's guide.

  2. **Cutting your losses:** Similarly, you want to be ready to cut your losses if a trade goes too wrong while also not getting out too early in case the cryptocurrency recovers. Again, there are countless guides, YouTube videos and books to help you make this decision.

How to pick an exchange that's good for trading

If your primary goal with cryptocurrency is to actively engage in trades heavily, rather than buy it and hold on for dear life (HODL) for the long term, there are certain features you may want to look out for:

- **The currencies available:** Bitcoin to USD is widely available, but other fiat and cryptocurrencies might not be available at all exchanges.

- **Leverage available:** Leverage lets you trade beyond your initial deposit and multiply your gains, suiting those who prefer higher risks and higher rewards. You can often find leverage up to 20:1 with cryptocurrency, depending on your chosen platform and currency pair.

- **Trading features:** Hedging, stop-loss features and other options can give you more control over your trading. Experienced traders might be able to benefit from these, while first-timers might prefer to keep it simple.

- **Minimum purchase:** What's the minimum (and maximum) amount you can purchase? Does it work for you?

XIV. UNDERSTANDING OVER-THE-COUNTER (OTC) TRADING

If you're a trader who wants to purchase a large amount of cryptocurrency, buying coins or tokens through a traditional exchange exposes you to several problems. Not only can slippage greatly increase the cost of a trade, but you'll also need to deal with the risks of hacking and theft that come with trading on an ordinary exchange.

This is where over-the-counter (OTC) trading comes in. OTC trading is a service available to high-volume traders, meaning it's only available to certain individuals or groups. This guide will help you decide whether OTC trading is the right option for you, and what to look out for when deciding on an OTC solution. Let's dive in.

What is OTC trading?

OTC trading is cryptocurrency trading that takes place away from digital currency exchanges. As you will recall, these traditional exchanges act like stock exchanges: they're centralized platforms where buyers and sellers can trade cryptocurrencies based on current market prices. Buy and sell offers are made publicly available on an order book. The exchange then acts as the middleman between a buyer and a seller, and generally charges a fee for each transaction. Some of the best-known exchanges include Binance, Coinbase and BTC Markets.

Favored by many large-scale traders, trades on OTC exchanges are often placed by hedge funds, private wealth managers or high-net-worth individuals. OTC trades can be facilitated in several different ways, including the following:

- **Via brokers:** OTC trades are increasingly handled by brokers who specialize in large transactions. These platforms offer a personalized service to help high-volume traders execute large block trades and avoid problems with slippage by accessing funds through liquidity providers that hold large amounts of cryptocurrency. Examples of OTC brokers include itBit and HiveEx.com.

- **Through chat rooms:** The first major OTC trading of bitcoin took place in an IRC chatroom called #bitcoin-otc. This trading network is hosted on various IRC channels and allows peer-to-peer transactions between traders.

- **Using ATMs:** Bitcoin ATMs allow customers to convert their fiat currency into digital coins without needing to go through an online exchange.

Why would someone use OTC trading instead of a regular exchange?

Why would you bother with OTC trading when there's a huge variety of traditional cryptocurrency exchanges offering simple fiat-to-crypto transactions? There are several reasons why large-volume traders might consider going OTC:

- **Better prices:** The traditional (on-exchange) cryptocurrency market is still in its infancy, and there may not always be sufficient liquidity available on exchanges to process large trades. As a result, placing a substantial trade through a traditional exchange could move the price of a cryptocurrency in an unfavorable direction before your trade could be completed – this is known as slippage. Instead of being filled for a single price, large orders can end up being spread over several smaller orders, with the price of each order often increasing. OTC trading allows traders to access one price for a single buy order.

- **Avoid low trading limits:** Most traditional exchanges place a limit on the maximum amount a user can trade per day as well as on the amount that can be withdrawn from an account in a 24-hour period. These limits can also vary based on factors such as the transaction methods used, the level of account verification completed and how long a user has been trading with the platform. In many cases, they may be insufficient to meet the needs of large-scale traders.

- **Quicker trading times:** Depending on the liquidity available, large trades can take days to be completed on a traditional exchange. Using OTC trading can guarantee faster processing times.

- **Use a trusted broker:** There have been numerous examples of traditional cryptocurrency exchanges being targeted by, and all too frequently falling victim to, hacking attacks. Placing OTC trades through a trusted broker allows you to avoid this risk.

What is slippage?

Slippage is when a cryptocurrency price changes while an order is being filled, resulting in a different price than what was initially expected for a trade. It's a common drawback associated with placing larger trades on traditional exchanges since insufficient liquidity on an exchange - as in, available cryptocurrency to be traded - can lead to a single order being split into several smaller orders.

Before all of those smaller orders can be filled, the price could shift in an unfavorable direction, resulting in a more expensive purchase than originally desired.

OTC trading vs trading cryptocurrency on an exchange

Not sure if you're the type of trader who could benefit from OTC trading? Check out the list of pros and cons when comparing OTC trading with buying coins on a traditional exchange to work out whether it's right for you.

Pros

- Designed for large-scale trades, either for high-net-worth individuals or for institutional traders .

- Allows you to avoid slippage, which may result in a better price.

- Avoids hacking risks associated with cryptocurrency exchanges.

- Allows you to deal with a trusted broker.

- Often offers a faster settlement of large trades and quicker access to your funds than exchange-based transactions.

- Also a viable option for ICOs looking to convert crypto earned from their projects into fiat currency.

Cons

- May have higher fees than traditional exchanges.

- OTC trading can't be automated through an API just as we've seen with the more traditional exchange trading.

- Only for large-scale investors, so not an option for small traders.

- If using a broker, you'll need to trust the broker to thoroughly vet counterparties before trading.

- Higher level of settlement risk than traditional exchange-based trading.

- Trading directly on an exchange may be more beneficial for those who want to actively trade price movements.

Case Study

In the Global Cryptocurrency Exchange Trends report, released by HiveEx.com in March 2018, the authors compared the cost of buying $300,000 worth of bitcoin (BTC) with the cost of the same transaction on HiveEx.com's OTC service.

On the regular cryptocurrency exchange, it took 46 separate transactions to fill the order and, after fees had been deducted, resulted in 34.31 BTC being purchased. On the OTC platform, only one trade was required and resulted in the purchase of 35.03 BTC for the same amount. This 0.72 BTC difference between the two providers equated to $6,464.88 as of 10 a.m. on March 21, 2018. This therefore demonstrates the OTC provider as the cheaper option in this case.

How OTC transactions work

The first step in any OTC transaction is finding a counterparty for the trade. This could be done through a chat room such as the #bitcoin-otc network, but is more commonly done through an OTC brokering platform.

The next step is to negotiate the terms of the trade. If you're looking to buy BTC, for example, you may wish to specify the following; the amount of BTC you want to buy, when you want the trade to take place and your desired price.

The seller will then respond with their offer price for the transaction, which will often be expressed as a percentage above a leading exchange's best available price – for example, Exchange A + 1%. Of course, the exact negotiation process will vary depending on whether you're the buyer or the seller, the medium you're using to arrange the trade, the size of the transaction and whether you have any leverage.

Once a price has been agreed upon, the buyer sends a bank transfer to the seller to cover the purchase price, and the seller sends the relevant amount of crypto coins or tokens to the buyer. Depending on where both parties involved in the trade reside, they may also need to complete KYC (Know Your Customer) due diligence on each other to make sure they satisfy legal requirements.

How popular is OTC trading?

Quantifying the amount of OTC trading that takes place on cryptocurrency markets is more or less impossible. This is due to the fact that these trades aren't publicly reported or independently audited. However, there is an increasing number of OTC brokers and platforms with public profiles, along with plenty of evidence to suggest the presence of large-scale trades.

For example, in the HiveEx.com report above, analysis of data from BitInfoCharts revealed that the average trade value of BTC on March 20, 2018 was $49,258. Now this was despite the fact that half of all bitcoin trades were less than $645.29. This demonstrates that large trades are bringing up the average value away from the median.

What about dark pools?

An in-depth look into OTC crypto trading raises the sinister-sounding topic of dark pools, which are designed to allow large-scale traders to transact with one another away from traditional exchanges.

Dark pools are basically private order books that are not visible to the rest of the market, allowing "whales" and institutional traders to trade anonymously. Not only does this allow them to avoid slippage caused by large trades, it also allows them to keep their trading activities confidential.

Users typically need to meet a minimum liquidity requirement to participate in these dark pools, thereby putting them out of reach of the general public.

The demand for the underground liquidity that dark pools offer is not unique to crypto markets, but the number of cryptocurrency dark pools is increasing. Cryptocurrency exchange Kraken launched a dark pool in 2015, online broker TradeZero introduced a bitcoin dark pool in 2016 and Republic Protocol made headlines in February 2018 when its ICO raised $30 million to create a decentralized dark pool for the atomic trading of bitcoin, Ether and ERC20 altcoin tokens.

What features should I look for in an OTC broker?

There's an increasing range of OTC trading desks available, so make sure to consider the following features when comparing your options:

- **Transaction amounts:** What are the minimum and maximum trade amounts the dealer can help you arrange? Do these fit with your trading needs?

- **Fees:** How much will you be charged in fees on each transaction you make? Is there a simple flat fee or does the amount vary based on the size of the trade and your personal circumstances?

- **Sign-up process:** What do you need to do to sign up for an account with this OTC broker? Are there know your customer or anti-money laundering requirements you need to fulfill?

- **Supported currencies:** Check a list of all the cryptocurrencies the broker can help you purchase? Is it limited to major currencies like bitcoin, Ether and Ripple, and are there any currencies missing that you'd like to acquire?

- **Security and storage:** How does the broker store client assets? What sort of protective measures does it have in place to ensure the security of client funds?

- **Customer support:** Will you receive personalized support and assistance from start to finish of the transaction? How can you get in touch with the broker if you ever have any questions or problems?

- **Reputation and reviews:** How long has the broker been in business? Do they specialize solely in OTC trading, or do they also offer other services? How do other users rate their service?

By considering the above and other factors, you'll be able to make a more informed decision when choosing an OTC broker.

XV. STEP-BY-STEP GUIDE FOR CONVERTING ONE CRYPTOCURRENCY TO ANOTHER

If you're going to dive deep into the cryptocurrency world, chances are you're more likely to want to trade a cryptocurrency whose value is dropping for one whose value is rising in order to protect your profits. So let's consider the step-by-step guide from chapter XI, but imagine we branched off at Step 8 as follows.

1. (Starting at step 8 from chapter IX): After proceeding with the payment, you now have 1.576 LTC in your exchange wallet, and you go to bed wondering what the next day may bring.

2. When you awake in the morning, you discover that LTC has mooned following a big announcement from the CEO. The value of your LTC had jumped 30% and at one point you had $130 in your wallet on your chosen exchange. Nice trading!

3. However, you begin to notice that the value of LTC is dropping as other traders begin to sell-off their winnings. At $120, you decide to withdraw the profits, $20 worth of LTC, and store that in a desktop wallet.

4. You find a desktop wallet that accepts LTC, looks reputable and has good reviews. You download it, install it and set it up – receiving its unique key. You return to your exchange, find the "withdraw" button and ask that $20 worth of LTC be sent to your desktop wallet address for safe keeping.

5. Once complete, and following a small fee, you now have $98 worth of LTC left in the exchange's wallet. However, its value is still dropping. You examine the latest prices, which are available on the finder website, and notice that another coin, Cardano (ADA), is on the up. You've read about (and like the look of) Cardano and since it's risen from $0.42 to $0.53 in the past hour, you decide you want to convert your LTC holdings into ADA.

6. You click on the "sell" button on your exchange, and look for the option to convert LTC/ADA (or it may be written as ADA/LTC). You then sell 100% (or $98) of your LTC at the current market rate, and request to buy $96 of ADA at the current sell rate. (You lose $2 in transaction fees along the way.)

7. With your transaction lodged, the exchange looks to other transaction requests to see if it can find a buyer for your LTC, and someone selling ADA. When a match is found, the transaction is confirmed by the miners on both the blockchains, and the request is fulfilled.

8. At this point, you now own $98 worth of ADA, which is worth approximately 185 ADA coins at the aforementioned value of $0.53. Unfortunately, the price of LTC has continued to drop in the interim, and the $20 in LTC you have in your desktop wallet is now only worth $15 – but you're saving that for the long haul, hoping it will rise over time.

NOTE: At Step 6, we showed how you might typically swap between cryptocurrencies on a single exchange, but in many cases the altcoin you want may not be on the exchange you are using. So what happens then? You will need to find an exchange that has the altcoin you are after, sign up to it and go through the verification process. At the end of this, you will receive a new online wallet on that new exchange. You can then withdraw the LTC from your first exchange's wallet and send it to the digital code for your new exchange's wallet. Once you've moved that LTC across to the new exchange, you can trade it for ADA as noted in the rest of the steps above.

Of course, the sign-up process is lengthy, so at the first time of asking, it's hard to capitalize on this kind of market movement quickly enough to catch the rising value. But for the sake of this case study example, you can still understand the process.

XVI. WHERE CAN YOU USE CRYPTOCURRENCY

In the above chapters, we've taken you through what cryptocurrency is, how to get it and how to trade it, but what if you wanted to use it? There are a few different ways to use cryptocurrencies today, and no doubt many more ways will emerge in the future.

For their intended purpose: If nothing else, you can always use a cryptocurrency exactly as it was originally intended. For bitcoin, this might be simply holding onto it or using it to buy other cryptocurrencies. For Ethereum, this might be powering smart contracts, which consumes small amounts of Ether as a sort of transaction fee. For Ripple, it might be to send money across borders in the blink of an eye and for a miniscule fee. And for the 1,000+ other cryptocurrencies in existence, this might be almost anything.

Purchase products or services: Are you paying with cash, credit or cryptocurrency? A lot of merchants today accept popular cryptocurrencies as payment, especially if you're paying with a popular currency like bitcoin. These merchants might be as small as someone selling used furniture on Craigslist or as big as Microsoft. In brick-and-mortar stores that accept cryptocurrency, you'll often see QR codes printed and pinned next to the cash registers. These are scanned to make crypto payments.

We've also begun to see working examples of people withdrawing fiat money from ATMs or paying for goods at a supermarket using a card that is connected to their digital wallet. This technology is only in its infancy, but points to a future where cryptocurrencies are as spendable and accessible as fiat money.

Some merchants have already made big wins out of using cryptocurrency. One of the most famous stories involves the rapper 50 Cent. He let people buy his album *Animal Ambition* with bitcoin back in 2014. Years later in 2018, 50 Cent was reminded of the fact by a fan who did just that and discovered that he had over $8 million in bitcoin due to its increase in value! How's your luck?

Money transfers and cryptocurrency tipping: Why would you use cryptocurrency to send someone money? The real question is why wouldn't you. Some cryptocurrencies are specifically designed to make transfers as quick and cheap as possible. For example, Nano (formerly RaiBlocks) lets you make 100% secure transfers in a couple of seconds flat without any fees whatsoever. Can your bank do that?

Or if you're sending money to someone who doesn't do crypto, you might use Stellar Lumens instead. This coin lets you make quick and cheap transfers while simultaneously converting money from cryptocurrency to your fiat currency of choice.

Transferring cryptocurrencies is often so quick and easy that some coins (like Dogecoin) have even built tipping platforms for themselves. With the press of a button, users tip each other with coins for entertaining or informative posts on Reddit, Twitter and other social media. That might not sound like a big deal, but blockchain technology marks the first time in history that people are able to send amounts as little as 5 or 10 cents to someone on the other side of the world. Previously these kinds of transfers would be eaten up by international transaction fees.

Trading opportunities: Despite all their applications, one of the main reasons people are buying cryptocurrencies is to try and make money. The enormous ups and downs that characterize the volatile cryptocurrency market have made it a playground for traders of different types.

- **Short term:** Cryptocurrencies are extremely volatile and move very fast. A trader who learns to predict (or create) these market movements can make a lot of money by buying low and selling high. They can also lose a lot of money if things go wrong.

- **Long term:** Buyers who believe in the future of a coin can buy and hold for the long run in hopes of seeing their initial purchase multiply over and over again.

- **Futures traders:** Regulated futures trading has come to cryptocurrency. Traders can go long or short on specific coins, trade with leverage and profit from crypto without buying any coins of their own.

XVII. WHAT TO WATCH OUT FOR

Cryptocurrencies are not without their pitfalls and you will need to be careful when handling your digital currency to avoid losing everything you own. Before jumping into cryptocurrency, do your research. No one guide will ever be able to cover everything you need to know about all cryptocurrencies, and you'll always be able to find two sides to any argument. Additionally, understand how exchanges and wallets work.

Before you make a decision, make sure you're informed. Read guides, find reviews and test drive with small, disposable amounts of money before making bigger purchases. Be aware that there is no safety net when working with cryptocurrencies. It's still largely unregulated and you typically won't be able to make a police report if your cryptocurrency gets stolen. The freedom to go beyond the banks and outside of government money comes with a lot of responsibility. Here are a few tips:

- Before you send cryptocurrency to someone, you should always double check their wallet address.

- Never hand over products or services before the transaction on the blockchain has been verified. This might take up to ten minutes on some blockchains.

- Always keep the computer where your wallet is installed safe and clean from viruses and malware.

- Never lose your wallet password. You might not be able to get it back and you will lose all of your cryptocurrency.

As we've touched on previously, don't forget that bitcoin and cryptocurrencies in general often suffer from sudden dips in value. Whenever purchasing cryptocurrency, always be aware that the value of your holdings can fall. For example, if you buy $1,000 worth of bitcoin one day at $5,871.92/BTC and the price falls to $5,770.54 the next day, your 0.170302 BTC will be worth $982.73 instead of the original $1,000 you paid for it.

Of course, this could work in your favor if it goes the other way round. However, always be aware that the cryptocurrency market is extremely volatile and past performance is not indicative of future performance.

Crypto and Tax

They say there are two sure things in life, one of them taxes. Unfortunately, nobody gets a pass — not even cryptocurrency owners. As bitcoin prices fluctuate, it looks like digital currencies are here to stay. But it's increasingly falling under the purview of the taxman.

It's hard for us to give too much advice in this book, given tax is a very country-specific topic. That said, we have detailed information for you to read on the finder.com.au website for Australian readers and on the finder.com website for American readers, should you come from those regions.

In general, however, if you've bought and sold cryptocurrency in the last financial year, it's time to start thinking about the impact this may have on your income tax return. If you've made a profit from trading in cryptocurrency, it's likely you'll need to declare it in your annual return.

Depending on your country of residence, here are the typical ways that your government may want to tax your cryptocurrency activity:

- **Investing in cryptocurrency:** If you hold any digital currency as an investment, you could be taxed on the capital gains you make when you sell it for a fiat currency or another crypto.

- **Trading cryptocurrency:** If you trade crypto for profit, you're likely to need to include those profits as part of your assessable income for tax purposes.

- **Mining cryptocurrency:** Any profits you make mining bitcoin or any other cryptocurrency will likely form part of your assessable income.

- **Carrying on a business:** If your business pays for goods and services using cryptocurrency, or receives payments for goods and services in cryptocurrency, these transactions could be subject to tax implications.

- **Running a crypto exchange:** If you operate a crypto exchange service, income tax often applies to the profits you make and your transactions could be subject to tax.

There are other things you need to consider as well. In some situations you may be able to claim a loss as an expense, for example, depending on how that loss occurred. You may also be subject to different taxation processes depending on whether you are into crypto as an investor or as a trader.

This latter point is an area where the documentation by governments is still being worked out. There's a lack of concrete information on what constitutes the difference between a cryptocurrency investor and a cryptocurrency trader. Perhaps looking to the traditional finance sector could help and how the question; "Shareholding as investor or share trading as business?" is answered.

While a shareholder is someone who owns shares with the purpose of earning income from dividends, a share trader is someone who carries out business activities to earn income from buying and selling shares. Working out which category you fall into is determined by evaluating numerous factors:

- The nature of the activity (are you trying to turn a profit?)

- The repetition, volume and regularity of the activities (how often and how much do you trade?)

- Whether you're organised in a business-like way (for example, do you have a business plan, business premises, accounts and records of trading stock etc?)

- The amount of capital you've invested.

We must point out, however, we're not tax experts, and general information such as that found in this guide is no substitute for professional advice. Consider your own situation and circumstances before relying on the information laid out here. And be sure to reference your country's official government documentation.

XVIII. THE HISTORY OF CRYPTO PONZI GAMES

Cryptocurrency Ponzi games have a long (at least by cryptocurrency standards) and fascinating history. Despite being scams – often transparently so – they still managed to find an audience of willing investors. The best way to understand cryptocurrency Ponzi schemes is to examine their history.

Famous scam artist Bernie Madoff would be proud. His popular FOMO3D Ponzi game is sitting on over 35 million dollars' worth of Ether, while its copycats and imitators are pulling in millions more. It's been a long and fascinating road to get this far though, and open and transparent Ponzi scheme games have been a staple of cryptocurrency for a while now. These are projects that openly describe themselves as Ponzi schemes and explicitly tell users how it all works.

At its heart, the idea behind the Ponzi games, as well as scams themselves which don't openly admit to being Ponzi schemes, is simply for people to deposit money into an account, and then get back more than they deposited. The game ends when there are no longer enough new deposits to pay out the most recent participants.

A brief history of crypto Ponzi games

It's worth walking through a brief history of transparent cryptocurrency Ponzi games, if you're into that kind of thing.

2011: Bitcoin Ponzi games emerge

Open bitcoin Ponzi games have been going on since at least 2011, and people seem to have had a lot of fun playing with different rule sets (higher or lower payouts, letting players choose the fees for the next person in line, different minimum and maximum deposits, etc.) to try to create the catchiest Ponzi scheme around and enrich everyone at the expense of the unlucky punters who get caught holding the bag at the end.

At its heart, Ponzi games of any kind are similar to more widely-played games such as pass the parcel, musical chairs or buying a house in 2007.

But overall, the early ones might be best thought of as online trust fall games (where a person deliberately falls, relying on others known as spotters to catch them). People deliberately fall by sending money to a stranger, and then trust others to catch them by sending even more money to the same stranger. And everyone trusts the game's creator not to exit the scam on them and run off with all the money.

2014: The next generation

The games have evolved over the years and across bitcoin's ups and downs. However, it got kicked up a distinct notch in 2014. This was shortly after bitcoin's first foray above the $1,000 mark, which injected a lot more money and interest into the space. It was also around this time that PonziCoin arrived; an automated Ponzi game that brought trustlessness to the system. With increasingly large amounts of money at stake, it got more important to programmatically remove the possibility of exit scams and create transparently fair Ponzi games.

The first PonziCoin met an untimely end when its funds abruptly disappeared after a month in operation. Initial speculation was that the game's owner had run off with the money, and that PonziCoin might have been a scam.

The founder later said the game's website was hacked, and that it was time to put the thing to bed. The game turned over around $126,000 in its lifetime, assuming average bitcoin prices of $600 for the duration of its operation, and lost $7,000 in the disappearance. The bitcoin churned through the game is naturally worth millions these days.

It was one of the larger Ponzi games at the time, but it's still a far cry from the US$50 million-odd frenzy currently going on around FOMO3D There's also the chart-topping PoWH3D and other related Ponzi games.

2015: Ethereum arrives

Then Ethereum arrived in 2015, coming into existence against a long backdrop of niche-yet-popular Ponzi games. Its smart contract functionality allowed for more Ponzi game possibilities, while the ability to easily create new tokens that can simply run on Ethereum's blockchain, rather than needing to develop their own consensus network, allowed for the creation of separate Ponzi game cryptocurrencies for the first time.

Now it was possible to actually create an entire Ponzi economy of sorts, and for Ponzi game money to be traded on an open market for other cryptocurrencies. These exciting new possibilities, in combination with the growth in the cryptocurrency user base, saw even more money get involved.

Several new PonziCoins have emerged and forked off the popular Ethereum blockchain over time, taking varying forms.

UET: Free market Ponzi

The Useless Ethereum Token (UET) was one of them, plying the exact same model without explicitly referring to itself as a Ponzi game. It went through an ICO and promised "investors" that they would be getting exactly nothing except worthless tokens in return. The value, if you can call it that, held by the UET tokens would be determined entirely by market forces rather than the game.

The distribution itself was gamified along gambling lines, with growing returns for larger "investments" and a 1 in 256 chance of ICO contributors winning a jackpot of even more useless tokens during their purchase.

UET was a hit, with its ICO pulling in about $150,000 worth of Ether. Its market performance since then – UET/ETH pairs are still traded on exchanges like HitBTC – has been about on par with most other ICOs. Incidentally, vulnerabilities allow hackers to pull UET out of people's wallets, which probably shouldn't come as a surprise given that the creator explicitly said gaping vulnerabilities were a definite possibility.

The former Ponzi game champion

The next Ethereum PonziCoin, which cropped up shortly after UET arrived, did even better. It was also called PonziCoin, like its 2014 predecessor, but ran its own separate Ethereum token. It ran its own unique and interesting twist on the classic Ponzi scheme, taking advantage of Ethereum's functionality and separate ETH market to programmatically adjust coin prices in line with demand.

Basically, people could put money into the PonziCoin contract to buy PONZI coins. The contract allowed people to trade Ether for PONZI as well as trade PONZI for Ether at a quarter of the price they initially purchased it for. The trick is that the value of PonziCoin would automatically increase based on how much money was put into it, so anyone who gets in early enough can profit if the price rises more than fourfold.

Like a classic Ponzi scheme or multi-level marketing system, the goal was to encourage buyers to get in early and then pressure others into purchasing. PONZI buyers were also treated to a message saying "also we need to be competitive with CryptoKitties' cuteness so here's a really nice dog" if they were brave enough to have a punt.

The game was a definite hit, pulling in around 250 Ether valued at more than $250,000 at the time, within just the first eight hours. This spooked the heck out of the creator who just wanted to have a laugh, then realised it was making so much money that they might have accidentally crossed the line into running a literal Ponzi scheme and actually committing fraud. They swiftly announced that it had gotten out of hand and shut the game down before it got too crazy.

Over the years, those fun bitcoin trust fall games with pretend money had gotten very real and started dealing with serious money, even as the games remained largely the same. They've become a serious part of the industry.

FOMO3D: The new Ponzi game champion

FOMO3D has now blown away all old records, and as of late July 2018, it held about 75,000 ETH worth - around US$35.5 million. It's very much in a league of its own, and the money put into it has also spawned a series of copycats worth about another $15 million, some of which are actual scams as opposed to just scam-themed games.

The essence of FOMO3D is that people can buy keys with Ether. The keys add time to the countdown timer. Each key increases the timer by 30 seconds up to a maximum of 24 hours. If no one buys a key before the timer runs out, the game ends, and that multi-million dollar pot is distributed among the various winners.

A player joins one of four different teams, but still competes individually. The teams instead affect how a player's resources are distributed between the keys, the P3D tokens and the exit scam itself.

The following are the three types of keys, tokens and events:

1. **FOMO3D keys:** These are the bread and butter of the game. The purchase of these keys prevents the exit scam event by adding 30 seconds to the timer per key purchased. If the timer runs out, the last person to buy keys can choose to "exit scam" and take the entire pot, minus the portion given to other players based on their key purchases, and the round ends.

   The Ponzi element comes from the price scaling, which raises the price of keys the longer a round continues. So someone who buys up a lot of cheap keys early on might net a very tidy profit, especially when a round gets as rich as this one is. Plus, every key purchase of 0.1ETH or more has a chance of winning some of the airdrop pot as a kind of door prize to encourage purchases.

2. **P3D tokens:** These dividend-paying tokens are like a stake in the game itself, and they don't reset each round. Instead, they pay out dividends taken from the 10% fee charged for transactions in the game. So far it's paid out over 35,000 ETH to P3D buyers. P3D tokens can be bought and sold at any time, but it costs 10% more to buy them due to the fees.

3. **The Exit Scam:** This happens when the timer runs out. This is when the total pot for the round is distributed, with the last key buyer getting the lion's share, but all key buyers receiving some amount based on how many keys they have.

The mid-2018 pot was up to about 21,500 Ether, worth about $10.3 million. At this time, it rarely went a couple of seconds without topping up back to 24 hours, so it's probably going to be a while before the pot is actually won. With so much money on the line, and so much more coming in, it might be possible that this round never actually ends for as long as Ethereum exists.

In response to this problem, and to keep new buyers coming in, the team behind this game is planning to release a short version with set round timers in the near future.

The future of Ponzi games

You don't have to look very far to find vocal criticisms of crypto Ponzi games, and various voices dismissing them as "a new level of stupidity."However, a very brief moment of consideration makes it clear that they have a lot more in common with traditional gambling than they do with actual Ponzi schemes, the same way movie-themed slot machines (of which there are a lot) are still just pokie machines rather than cinematic experiences.

But like many traditional areas redone with a crypto twist, Ponzi games are able to bring in new elements of trustless profit-sharing among users, interesting angles around community management and economic theory, and the notion of trust, especially in the early days of bitcoin Ponzi games. By mistakenly thinking of Ponzi games as actual scams, one misses out on a lot of interesting developments and potential for future development.

Games like FOMO3D are the natural intersection of gambling and cryptocurrency, and the reason FOMO3D is so popular is probably just because it's a catchy game that people want to play, rather than because the world has gone mad, kids are crazy these days or similar. And like all the other areas it stands to disrupt, cryptocurrency still has a very long way to go before it even comes close to touching the expenditure of traditional variants.

USA state lotteries, for example, pulled in $80.5 billion in ticket sales in 2016. And Australian slot machines used to do about $11 billion per year before the country collectively said "woah" and pulled back a bit. And actual fiat Ponzi schemes are still historically much more lucrative than crypto scams. Madoff's record will hopefully stand for a while.

Games like FOMO3D are one example among many of cryptocurrencies putting a new twist on old ideas. Ponzi games are an especially great example of this because they transparently highlight some of the bizarre ways money can be contorted. Plus, you can still enjoy the ride from a safe distance without knowingly dropping any of your own money into a Ponzi.

XIX. MEET THE TOP COINS

Over the coming pages, we are going to take you through the most notable cryptocurrency coins on the market as of the start of 2018. This is determined by their market capitalization. Market capitalization refers to the total value of all the coins from that cryptocurrency that are available on the market. So this doesn't include coins that have been burned, which means they have been deemed unspendable by the creator, or locked out of the public trading market for private use.

As of the start of 2018, there was US$430 trillion dollars' worth of cryptocurrency held in the public market across all the coins. That figure is referred to as the total market cap. The top 10 coins account for 80% of that cap, and 90% is held in the top 30. While the market cap for all the coins changes daily, the top 20 have been pretty solidly in place for quite some time now, with the coins below that seeing the most change in and out of the top 50 over the course of any day.

Of course, there is only one place to start...

A – BITCOIN

Symbol: *BTC, XBT*
Initial release date: *January 3, 2009*
Encryption algorithm: *SHA-256*
Max. supply: *21 million BTC*
Est. total market cap ownership: *35%*

It's impossible to talk about cryptocurrencies without talking about bitcoin. Starting from very humble origins and with a view to disrupting government control over public finances, bitcoin has grown to become a powerhouse in the financial sector. More and more merchants, businesses and even governments are adopting the coin, and the blockchain technology behind it, in ways the creator of bitcoin couldn't have imagined.

We have covered a lot of the bitcoin basics already over the earlier sections of this guide. It's "use case" for existing as a cryptocurrency is the blockchain itself and it is the founding father of cryptocurrencies.

Bitcoin started as a paper authored by bitcoin's creator Satoshi Nakamoto, titled "A Peer-to-Peer Electronic Cash System" (2008). In it, Satoshi, whose real identity remains unknown at the time of writing in October 2017, details a system for decentralizing the financial sector, with the aim of giving power back to the people via an entirely digital transaction system (which would later become known as the blockchain). In January 2009, the first block was mined by Satoshi for 50 bitcoin. While still directly involved in the development of bitcoin, Satoshi is rumored to have mined nearly one million bitcoin, an amount that would, just eight years later, be worth upwards of US$5.8 billion.

The creation of the blockchain

Satoshi's vision for bitcoin began from a very simple concept: we don't need a centralized agency controlling our money (i.e., the central bank). To accomplish this, bitcoin needs to be maintained by the people using the cryptocurrency, and it does so by using a public ledger, more commonly known as the blockchain. Understanding the blockchain will help you understand the finer points of the currency.

Imagine three people: Alice, Bob and Charlie. They often have to pay money to each other, but to avoid having to make a payment every time they need to, they decide to start keeping a ledger of money owed. At the end of the month, they work out who is owed what and pay them. To avoid having to trust each other with this ledger, they bring on Daryl, a third party who's been entrusted with maintaining the ledger's integrity. The ledger might look something like this:

Alice > Bob =	$10
Bob > Charlie =	$25
Bob > Alice =	$15
Charlie > Alice =	$55
Charlie > Bob =	$12

Every bitcoin transaction is stored in a digital ledger like that one. Each line signals a sending address, a receiving address and an amount of bitcoin (BTC, but read our later comment about XBT). There is also some additional security information to ensure the addresses are correct. Each set of transactions is stored on a block, like a page in a ledger. Once a block is filled with transactions, it can be mined by miners (see chapter III) and is then attached to the previous block to form a chain of such pages or blocks: a blockchain.

To instill some sense of anonymity in the blockchain, bitcoin does not hold the personal information of either the sender or receiver in blockchain transactions. Instead, each user gets a public address (a.k.a. a wallet address) and these addresses are stored for the transaction instead. Once a transaction is added to a block, and a block is added to the blockchain, it is said to be immutable: it can neither be edited nor deleted. To understand why, let's next take a look at decentralization.

The problem with this ledger system is readily apparent when we introduce some malice. If Daryl were to cut a deal with, say Charlie, and put in a new transaction showing Alice and Bob owing Charlie money, Alice and Bob are now in the difficult situation. They either have to pay the owed money, trusting Daryl, or refute the idea of the ledger altogether.

Alice > Bob	$10
Bob > Charlie	$25
Bob > Alice	$15
Charlie > Alice	$55
Charlie > Bob	$12
Alice > Charlie	$100
Bob > Charlie	$100

To solve this problem, all three participants in our experiment now decide to keep a copy of the ledger. If someone were to tamper with their copy of the ledger, we would simply have to compare it with the others and pick the most commonly consistent ledgers to use.

This is the second important solution provided by the blockchain. This consistency check is built into the blockchain techn – albeit with a little more complexity. Whenever you log into your copy of the ledger, you'll see a copy of every single transaction made with bitcoin since its inception and you will become part of this verification process. This democratization of verification lies at the heart of bitcoin and the blockchain process.

So Alice and Bob have an undoctored ledger reading:

Alice > Bob	*$10*
Bob > Charlie	*$25*
Bob > Alice	*$15*
Charlie > Alice	*$55*
Charlie > Bob	*$12*

And Charlie has a ledger reading:

Alice > Bob	*$10*
Bob > Charlie	*$25*
Bob > Alice	*$15*
Charlie > Alice	*$55*
Charlie > Bob	*$12*
Alice > Charlie	*$100*
Bob > Charlie	*$100*

As Charlie's ledger does not read like the majority, the transaction he alleges occurred will not be confirmed by miners and will not be appended to the block. Unless you can convince more than 50% of bitcoin users to remove a transaction for you, then that transaction is essentially set in stone.

Verification with bitcoin

The key problem bitcoin had to solve next is the idea of transaction verification. While there is no central authority that can decide whether a transaction is legitimate or fraudulent, there still needed to be a system for figuring this out. Bitcoin provides this solution via the act of mining. Miners, who are computer experts rather than people who work with pickaxes, do the complex work of mining.

Using powerful ASIC (Application-Specific Integrated Circuits) processors – which have a microchip specifically specialised for mining – miners receive a block of transactions and solve a computationally-difficult mathematical puzzle on that block. You'll remember our BUTTERFLY example from earlier in this book. Suffice to say, once solved, this puzzle guarantees that the transactions on the block are valid and can be considered verified.

Once mined, the miner solving the puzzle attaches the block to the blockchain and receives a small amount of bitcoin for the work. Mining today is highly competitive, and miners have to use the latest ASIC processors on the market, otherwise the cost of energy consumption to solve the puzzle outweighs the rewards.

Where can you use bitcoin?

Bitcoin is one of the (if not the) most widely accepted cryptocurrencies on the market as of the start of 2018. From online merchants to brick-and-mortar shops, many service providers have started accepting bitcoin along with fiat currency (i.e., regular currencies such as AUD, USD and EUR).

You can use bitcoin to purchase various products and services such as the following:

- **Electronics, software and gear:** Microsoft, Newegg and Dell, for example, all accept bitcoin payments.

- **Flights and travel amenities:** Expedia, one of the biggest travel agencies in the world, allows users to pay with bitcoin.

- **Casinos:** The bitcoin.com online casino launched in 2016 is completely anonymous and lets you play with bitcoin.

Apart from these big names, smaller merchants and service providers accept bitcoin.

Bitcoin's code: XBT OR BTC?

When reading about bitcoin, you will sometimes see it referred to as BTC and other times as XBT. So which one should you use? While BTC would appear to be winning the race come the start of 2018, the bitcoin community has not yet reached an official consensus.

Originally, bitcoin's currency code was BTC, but as it grew and gained widespread acceptance, the International Standards Organization (ISO) gave the currency a new code, "XBT", with the "X" representing the fact that bitcoin is not tied to a specific government (as per the ISO 4217 standard).

Many users of bitcoin still refer to the currency as BTC though, and this is not likely to change soon, even as use of XBT gains traction among bankers and financial advisors.

Can bitcoin be profitable?

Bitcoin, like other cryptocurrencies, is extremely volatile and the value of the currency remains unpredictable. News and seemingly unrelated events can have a big effect, either positively or negatively, on its price. This was particularly true from December 2017 to January to 2018, when cryptocurrency first went mainstream. Prices have levelled out since that time, but will it last? If you'd still like to take the plunge into bitcoin, there are two ways to do that:

1. **Get paid in BTC:** The fastest way to grow your wallet, bitcoin or otherwise, is to start getting paid with bitcoin. If you have an online shop, add a "pay with bitcoin" button to your shopping cart. As an online service provider, you might consider asking your clients whether they'd like to use bitcoin for payment. If you have a brick-and-mortar shop, you could print out your bitcoin wallet's address QR code and stick it next to the checkout so people will be able to scan it and send you bitcoin instantly. And if you're an employee, you can ask your employers if they'd be interested in paying your salary in bitcoin instead of fiat.

2. **Buy bitcoin:** If you'd like to play the bitcoin market, you can buy bitcoin and wait for your wallet to grow on its own. This works just like any other market trading process. You buy bitcoin from a reputable cryptocurrency exchange when the value is low and sell it when it's high. For example, if you had bought $10,000 worth of BTC on July 26, 2017, (3.92129183 BTC) and sold it three months later on October 21, 2017, for $23,579.63, you would have made over $13,500 profit and more than doubled your money.

   When it comes to trading bitcoin, keep in mind that past performance is not always an indicator of future performance, and with cryptocurrencies still in their infancy, large dips in value do occur.

How to get bitcoin

Sending and receiving bitcoin is a simple process as long as you've set up two things in advance of a transaction:

1. **An account on a digital currency exchange:** There are many currency exchanges available online from which you can purchase bitcoin. Check out our currency exchange on the finder website for information on how to choose the best one for your needs. After you've created an account and exchanged some fiat currency for bitcoin, the next step is to set up a wallet.

2. **A bitcoin wallet:** Again, there are many wallets you can use for bitcoin, and your best bet to choose one that fits your needs is to check the guide on the finder website. Once you're all set up, you're ready to start paying for products or services. Simply follow the instructions for your wallet of choice and you'll be trading bitcoin in no time.

What to watch out for

Bitcoin is not without its pitfalls, and many of those come from its perceived growth and wide acceptance. Because bitcoin is one of the most traded cryptocurrencies, it has attracted scammers and phishing websites, most in the form of exchanges. Before giving your money to an online exchange, make sure that it meets the following criteria:

- Uses HTTPS not HTTP.

- Requires identity verification.

- Has good reviews from reputable sources.

- Allows payments via credit cards and bank transfers (this way you'll be able to get help from the bank if it's a scam).

Even though bitcoin paved the way for all the other altcoins available on the market, some coins are doing things that are far more interesting than bitcoin. As of March 2018, Ethereum is riding hot on the heels of bitcoin with its far more innovative features built on the blockchain, including smart contracts and decentralized apps. This may be causing companies to pivot away from bitcoin and towards more exciting altcoins.

What's next for bitcoin?

Bitcoin has been around since 2009, but its future seems to be promising given the important changes coming its way.

SegWit upgrade: In 2017, the bitcoin community's main concern was how to better improve network performance and the length transaction times. As more and more users flock to bitcoin, performance time has suffered, causing the system to take too long to verify transactions. It could sometimes take up to 10 minutes to verify a transaction whereas other altcoins could do it in under a minute. This proposed software upgrade has been a long time coming, and it is hoped that this will result in faster verification times and even cheaper transaction fees.

Acceptance on the rise: Every day, more and more merchants are joining the bitcoin community. In all likelihood, this wider acceptance may be accompanied by some regulation from governments around the world. If this occurs, this might not be the killing blow that many bitcoin users fear. Regulation could provide some peace of mind to businesses and organizations that are still afraid of getting involved in cryptocurrencies.

Will transactions fees get better? The difficulty of mining a transaction, which is the required computational power to run the algorithm and solve the problem, determines the fee charged for fulfilling that transaction. That difficulty increases the more unconfirmed transactions are waiting in the queue. As bitcoin is the oldest blockchain and the most popular, its fees are the most extreme.

Bitcoin transaction fees hit a then-outrageous peak of US$20 on average on November 12, 2017. It smashed that unseemly record on December 8, 2017, and since then, its average transaction fees have been riding at over US$20.

It's not hard to see the connection between bitcoin prices, unconfirmed transactions and transfer fees. It's obvious enough that the high value of the coin is driving user uptake, which clogs up the network. But what's less obvious is just how immediate the correlation is. The correlation might be running in both directions too, with network difficulties keeping a lid on bitcoin prices. But will it get better?

It's safe to say that bitcoin will need to solve this problem if it wants to go further. The good news for traders is that the upcoming bitcoin Lightning Network update should help a lot. The bad news is that it might be better on paper than in practice.

The Lightning update is a major change for bitcoin. In oversimplified terms, it basically works by creating a whole new series of payment channels on the network that can be used instead of the main blockchain-based system. Peer-to-peer transactions on the Lightning Network can theoretically be done with almost non-existent transaction fees.

So instead of clogging up the blockchain by sending every single transaction through it, the bulk of them will run outside the blockchain entirely. However, the nodes that form the Lightning Network will be connected to the blockchain. Fees on the Lightning Network are paid to the node operators, and will be taken as a percentage of the transaction plus a slight fiat amount. This will facilitate microtransactions, but means it won't be much good for larger transactions. Those will stay on the current blockchain instead.

Theoretically, the Lightning Network could solve the current bitcoin transaction problems, but in the real world, it's not quite as easy. The first problem is that there's still no date for the Lightning Network rollout. It's currently undergoing testing, but it's almost certainly going to be months before it's ready for release.

The second problem is that once it is ready, it will require a willing uptake from bitcoin users. People will need to go out of their way to actually set up those Lightning nodes and start using it. The scale of this obstacle can't be overstated. Consider SegWit (Segregated Witness). This update was released in August 2017 to reduce the amount of data involved in each transaction. Essentially, you can fit more SegWit transactions onto one block. This improves transaction times and reduces fees.

But half a year later and with the bitcoin network slowed to a crawl, fewer than 10% of transactions actually bother with SegWit. This is because it's a bit of a hassle and requires some additional steps to use. Bitcoin in general isn't the easiest-to-use currency, especially for newcomers, so a layer of complication like SegWit naturally goes unused. It's very clear that simply having a viable solution isn't enough. People actually need to start using it.

Plus, the Lightning Network actually requires SegWit in order to work. The Lightning Network upgrade is still under construction and probably won't be ready for months. But even if was ready to go today, people still wouldn't be using it.

If it is adopted and works as advertised, another question raises its head: if bitcoin gets "fast," what happens to the altcoins that have "fast" as a main selling point. It's a topic we debate on the finder website.

You can get the latest bitcoin price on the finder website.

B – ETHEREUM

Symbol: *ETH*
Initial release date: *July 30, 2015*
Encryption algorithm: *Ethash*
Max. supply: *Unlimited*
Est. total market cap ownership: *19%*

If you've been involved in any way with cryptocurrencies, you've probably heard of Ethereum. Ethereum began out of a need to see bitcoin's underlying technology, the blockchain, used for something greater than simply sending currency from one user to another. Vitalik Buterin, the creator of Ethereum, built the system to be a "world computer" incorporating a virtual machine (EVM), a Turing-complete programing language (Solidity, Viper), a token (ETH) and fuel (gas).

But we're getting ahead of ourselves.

When most people talk about Ethereum, they are really talking about Ether (ETH), the underlying currency of the Ethereum platform. This confusion stems from the fact that bitcoin and its underlying technology, the blockchain, were never really defined separately when bitcoin launched. The idea was that the blockchain would be little more than the system that allows the transfer of BTC between users, and Satoshi, the creator of bitcoin, intentionally limited the blockchain's capabilities for security purposes. But the coin and the blockchain are two very different things, acting and used independently.

So while you will not see the words bitcoin and blockchain used interchangeably, given their disparate meanings, Ether and Ethereum often are. This occurs despite Ether being the equivalent of bitcoin and Ethereum being the equivalent of the blockchain technology.

Ether, traded under the code ETH, can be purchased at exchanges and used to pay for products and services at most merchants that accept cryptocurrencies. After all, it's the second biggest cryptocurrency by market cap as of March 2018. Ether is also used to pay for transaction fees and for computational services when using the Ethereum network.

Ether is mined similarly to bitcoin. You set your computer so that it attempts to solve the question present on a particular block in the blockchain. Once you find the answer, you get paid in Ether.

However, the goal of Ethereum is to be something greater than "just another altcoin." Not happy with how blockchain technology was being underutilized by bitcoin, the creators of Ethereum set out to take the blockchain to the next level. They envisaged a method to decentralize the Internet itself.

How does Ethereum look at decentralization?

We've spoken about it at length in previous chapters, but let's quickly summarize the concept of a centralized system. Let's say you have an online account where you store all your family photographs. Let's call it CloudPhoto. You can upload photos to CloudPhoto, and you can access those photos from anywhere. Now let's say something goes wrong, and CloudPhoto's servers melt. Unfortunately, you can't access your photos, and all of them are lost. This is a centralized system.

Usually, we mitigate this scenario by creating backups of our data. We make copies of the same data and store them elsewhere or keep different groups of data on different servers. This decentralizes the system.

Decentralization is also beneficial in cases where you need to maintain the integrity of data. For example, keeping all the student grades at a school on one computer is a problem because if someone hacks into that computer and changes those grades, then there would be no way to catch the change. If ten different computers held onto the student scores, it would be easy to recognize that one of the computers holding the data is wrong, and consequently fix that data set.

So a decentralized system is one where there is no single point of failure. And different from bitcoin, Ethereum aims to push the concept of decentralization to the broader applications of the Internet beyond finances. This has many obvious advantages, and you need to keep that in mind when considering Ethereum.

Ethereum virtual machine and dapps

Any software built using Ethereum technology is decentralized. These are referred to as decentralized applications, or dapps, and are the driving force behind Ethereum's development. In order for these dapps to use the Ethereum blockchain, they are run on the Ethereum virtual machine (EVM), also known as the World Computer. This is comparable to the concept of running software on the cloud.

This virtual machine is Ethereum's defining developmental discovery as it allows applications to run on the blockchain. Plus, the EVM, as a platform, is also Turing-complete. This means it can work on any machine capable of performing all conceivable programmable calculations (i.e., most modern computers). So you don't need a special computer in order to run the EVM, which allows anyone to become a node on the network. Dapps are coded in languages a normal computer can understand – most notably Solidity and Viper, two languages that share comparisons with JavaScript.

As previously mentioned, centralized systems suffer from single points of failures. If something were to happen to eBay, and they didn't have any backups, you would lose all evidence of your hard-earned success. Decentralized apps run on the blockchain and make use of it to maintain data scattered across all users of Ethereum. The data sets are, of course, encrypted so they are not accessible to everyone, but everyone would be able to verify and validate the data if the need arises.

There are already many dapps, ranging from online gambling programs to prediction markets and social media platforms, and most likely there are many more to come.

Gas-powered machine

Like all machines, the EVM needs fuel in order to be powered. Back in Chapter III, we talked you through the concept of mining, predominantly through the lens of bitcoin. We spoke about the idea of how confirming a transaction could become more or less difficult based on the computational power committed to the network versus the number of transactions attempting to be confirmed at any given time. The more difficult the confirmation, the greater the transaction fees as more effort needs to be put in by the miners.

Ethereum uses a different metric for measuring this difficulty, called gas. Each operation that needs to be confirmed on the EVM costs a certain amount of gas to be completed. If this is a simple transfer, the amount of gas required is low. But if it is a complex smart contract, the amount required can be much higher. Gas then, is effectively the fee charged to make a change by the network.

When you set about executing a change on the Ethereum network, you set the amount of gas you're willing to spend on getting it confirmed. In short, how much you are willing to reward Ethereum miners for solving the mathematical problem. This is referred to as the gas limit. Think of it like setting your highest bid price on eBay. The final price may not end up at that big amount, but you're willing to spend that much to get there.

Sadly, if you underestimate how much gas you need (i.e., you set the gas limit too low), the transaction will not be completed and the money you've spent on that gas will be lost. However, if you overestimate, you receive a refund of the remaining amount. The idea then of setting the gas limit at the time of a transaction is to establish your "fold" position, where you're not comfortable throwing any more money on the table to get the job done.

Adding to what is already a confusing system, gas itself has no specific monetary value. It's just a non-specific unit that shares a relationship to the number of units required to fill a block. However, you do nominate an ETH price in Gwei (which is the term given to fractions of an ETH coin – think of it as cents to ETH's dollar) that you are willing to pay for each unit of gas at the time of requesting the transaction. This gives the gas, your fee for the transaction, a value that can be passed on to the miner.

This gets us onto the second part of this equation. If we know that the units of gas represent the computation power required to solve that particular transaction, what then about the gas price? This is also set by the sender and is effectively a bid you make in order to encourage miners to confirm the transaction. Set it too low, and you will be waiting a long time to find miners willing to add you to the blockchain. Set it high, and you can get it verified very quickly indeed.

Thankfully, the price of gas and the amount of gas required to trade in ETH, as opposed to using the network for its third-party dapp functionality, isn't overly volatile. There are multiple portals online that track the average price in the market, so you can best predict the fees. The fees for a standard trade transaction as of the start of 2018 usually hovered around the $0.04 mark

If you're wondering why this gas system is used at all, it's to stop people from bogging down the Ethereum network with ridiculously huge computational problems to solve. It creates a scenario where it's in the best interest of a dapp creator to get the gas cost down, which in turn keeps the EVM running efficiently. This is a problem not faced by bitcoin, given it only deals with financial transactions, which are relatively simple mathematical problems to solve, and not smart contracts.

Plus, since a transaction has a limit, and that limit relates to the maximum amount of transactions that can be stored on a block, hackers can't set the network's nodes into an infinite loop and crash the system by tendering unsolvable mathematical problems. As soon as the problem reaches a certain gas requirement, it becomes too big to be appended to the blockchain and can therefore be ignored.

Smart contracts

If the EVM is how various people can use the Ethereum blockchain technology, it's smart contracts that form the basis of how that blockchain works. When a contract is written in computer code, as opposed to traditional legal language, it is deemed a smart contract. This programmed contract – think of it as an autonomous decentralized application – is set up to execute and carry itself out automatically under specified conditions. When a smart contract is on the blockchain, both parties can check its programming before agreeing to it, and then let it do its thing, confident that it cannot be tampered with or changed.

So it lets two parties agree to complex terms without needing to trust each other, and without needing to involve any third parties. Someone creates a contract with rules and triggers, both parties agree to that contract, and it then executes when the trigger event occurs – as long as all the rules can be enforced. This functionality is the defining feature of the Ethereum blockchain.

Smart contracts are one of the reasons everyone's so excited about cryptocurrencies and the blockchain. It's like having a robot that can do things automatically and can't be hacked or tampered with.

For example, someone could put $500 into an account guarded by a smart contract and set it up to send $5 to someone each year for their birthday over the next 100 years. They can do this with 100% certainty that the money will be sent exactly as programmed and with 100% certainty that no one can ever tamper with that program or steal the money.

Without smart contracts, you'd have to give the money to someone else and then trust them to send it onwards, even after you're gone. The decentralization of the blockchain system is what makes it 100% reliable and tamper-proof. But being able to program various functions into the blockchain, like sending $5 a year for 100 years, is the smart contract in action. That's what Ethereum added to what bitcoin began.

As you can imagine, smart contracts have enormous implications for businesses in almost any industry. A lot of the new cryptocurrencies being created these days are offering built-in smart contract technology.

The DAO hack

The Decentralized Autonomous Organization, or DAO, was to be the crown jewel of the Ethereum smart contract and virtual machine ecosystem. It was a smart contract that was going to build a decentralized venture capital fund with the aim of providing funding for all future dapp development. People would buy into the DAO, and they would be allowed to vote on which dapps got funding and which did not.

The DAO launched on April 30, 2016, and within 28 days, it had accumulated more than $150 million worth in ETH. The attack happened on June 17, 2016, and it worked by exploiting a loophole in the way buyers left the DAO. If you wanted to leave the DAO (as a buyer), you were allowed to take all the ETH you had put into the system after you returned the DAO tokens you had been given (a sort of stakeholder system).

The problem was that the contract had two steps. Step 1 involved taking DAO tokens from the user, and giving back ETH to the user. Step 2 involved registering the transaction in the blockchain and updating the DAO token count. The hack was simple in hindsight. Simply inject a step between Step 1 and Step 2 where, before the transaction gets registered, the DAO would give the same user more ETH for the same tokens.

This hack cost the DAO $50 million worth of ETH and caused the value of ETH to plummet from $20.17 to $11.52 in 48 hours.

Ethereum Classic (ETC) is a fork of Ethereum (ETH) that came about as a result of the way the developers and community behind Ethereum decided to handle the DAO attack. The majority of the Ethereum community agreed that the best course of action was to hold the money taken by the hacker, and return everything to the people who bought into the DAO, practically rewinding the hacker's attack.

So Ethereum's blockchain forked. In one fork, the blocks in the blockchain that occurred at the time of the DAO attack were removed from the record and the money returned to the wallets from which it had been originally transferred. This blockchain then continued on under the name Ethereum.

However, many Ethereum users did not agree with this as, in their opinion, it went against the core philosophy of cryptocurrencies that the blockchain is immutable and should not be affected by the whims of its users. Reverting the attack and forking the code to reset the blockchain went against the core philosophy that the code is law, and so many people stayed with the original blockchain, which became knowns as Ethereum Classic.

Where can you use ETH?

ETH has been on the rise since its inception and has been enjoying widespread acceptance by traders, exchanges and merchants. By the end of 2017, websites using cart software such as WooCommerce and OpenCart can be set up to accept ETH payments, and we will likely be seeing even more merchants popping up online that accept ETH.

But currently, the biggest use for ETH is as a stake in Ethereum. Perhaps that future will include a completely decentralized Internet where the centralized system of servers has become obsolete, returning power to the users themselves through the peer-to-peer blockchain system.

How do you get Ethereum?

There are many ways to get Ethereum. The simplest way is to buy some ETH and hold it. As more users buy ETH, more merchants will likely see the value of accepting ETH as payment, which may increase the value of the coin. An increase in the value of the coin would give more strength to the developers behind the Ethereum network and the dapps running on it, and this would in turn increase the value of your held assets.

Alternatively, you can buy into other platforms that use the Ethereum network. For examples, dapps that use the Ethereum network or other altcoins that forked out of

Ethereum, but are linked to its parent Ether's value. While not directly buying Ethereum, such trades are an endorsement of its use case and therefore indirectly add to its value.

What is ERC20?

By bringing the concept of smart contracts and dapps to blockchain technology, the Ethereum network has become a popular starting point for new coins. Ethereum is regularly forked into new altcoins that look to use or build upon the Ethereum technology in their own interesting ways. In a relatively recent development, Ethereum's developers decided to create a standard that all new coins using its network will need to meet. The developers hope this will create a more user-friendly, overarching ecosystem.

For example, think about all the different devices that use a USB port. They might be using media in different ways, but thanks to the USB standard, they can all connect to a PC in the same way. And as that standard improves, for example USB 3.0, all devices that make use of it gain that improvement.

Currently ERC30 specifies six functions, most of which are basic concepts such as how tokens are transferred and how users can access data about a token as well as signals that represent a token being part of the ETH ecosystem. This is all pretty straight-forward, like plugging something into a USB port and knowing it will work.

What to watch out for with Ethereum

Ethereum is trying to be bigger and better than simple cryptocurrencies like bitcoin, but the huge advantages it offers might also be its downfall. A platform is much harder to maintain, harder to develop and harder to encourage consistent adoption. A cryptocurrency is simple: buy and sell things using that currency. Bitcoin, for example, is nothing more than a currency and people, especially businesses and merchants, like simple things that just work.

Plus, with a roadmap as ambitious as Ethereum's, the journey is bound to be a little rocky. After all, platforms have failed for introducing far smaller, and far simpler, features that had unforeseen and sometimes fatal side-effects. This is obviously not a certainty, but it's good to be mindful of big changes coming in the future of Ethereum. Apart from a strong drive to have ETH accepted by more merchants, you can expect the biggest disruptions to occur in the dapps space.

You can find comparisons of exchanges that trade in Ether on the finder website. You can also read a review of the Ether wallet.

C – BITCOIN VS ETHEREUM

Bitcoin and Ethereum are the two biggest giants of the cryptocurrency world. Bitcoin (BTC) was the first coin and Ethereum (ETH) followed a few years later. We've just taken you through the details of each of these big players, which hold over 50% of the total market cap between them, but now we're going to compare them directly. After all, finder is a comparison website!

There are a lot of similarities between these two coins. Ethereum was initially created as a hard fork of bitcoin, so its programming is almost the same as its main rival. As detailed in the last chapter, the main difference is that ETH has built-in smart contract technology, which bitcoin doesn't.

What makes bitcoin and Ethereum similar?

There are a lot of similarities other than the programming between the two biggest coins.

- Both coins are valuable: At the time of writing, bitcoin and Ethereum are the top two coins, respectively, in terms of market cap. They're the world's biggest and most valuable cryptocurrencies by quite a stretch.

- **Both coins are popular:** Even with hundreds of other cryptocurrencies now in existence, bitcoin and Ethereum remain the most widely used.

- **Both coins are old:** Some of the newer coins outperform bitcoin and Ethereum in various ways. Other coins are quicker to transfer, have lower fees or have extra features. But none of them have such a sustained period of market confidence behind them.

- **Both coins use proof-of-work mining:** Mining is how transactions are processed on the blockchain. Back when bitcoin and Ethereum were created, proof-of-work mining was how all cryptocurrencies handled transactions. These days, not all coins use proof of work, and some coins don't even need mining.

- **Both coins have scaling problems.** Because they're so old, both bitcoin and Ethereum are having trouble with being too popular and having too many people using them. Having too many users means both can experience slower transactions and higher transaction costs than newer altcoins. To solve this, both are introducing their own different solutions to this problem.

Dealing with the scaling problem

Over the years, both bitcoin and Ethereum coins have differentiated themselves more and more from each other. However, it's their upcoming solutions to the scaling problem that could make that difference a massive abyss.

Bitcoin's solution: Over the years, bitcoin has had other hard forks that were specifically designed to solve its scaling problem. The Ethereum fork was designed to add smart contracts. But other hard forks were designed to make transactions faster and cheaper to help accommodate all the extra users that were arriving. Examples of these forks include Litecoin and Bitcoin Cash.

But bitcoin as we know it today resisted those hard forks and remained unchanged. Instead, it introduced a system called SegWit and has future plans of creating something called the Lightning Network.

- **SegWit:** A new way of arranging data to make transfers faster and easier. The downside is that you can only use SegWit with certain wallets and certain exchanges. This basically means that bitcoin users have to turn SegWit on and off to use it properly. If it's turned on or off at the wrong time when sending money, people risk losing their bitcoin. For this reason, most people just kept it turned off.

- **The Lightning Network:** A system that basically involves setting up multiple payment channels to go around the blockchain. The idea is to keep smaller transactions off the main bitcoin network. It's still under development.

Ethereum's solution: Ethereum's smart contracts are extremely useful, but can also slow down the network, especially when there are a lot of extremely complicated smart contracts with a lot of different steps. It needed different solutions. The planned updates to the Ethereum network include the following:

- **Plasma:** The Plasma update will only broadcast smart contracts to the main Ethereum blockchain after the contract's completion. Basically, it removes all the complicated and slow parts behind the scenes and only puts the final result on the main blockchain. This should prevent smart contracts, especially more complicated ones, from slowing down the network.

- **Casper:** This is a major change. It involves switching from the old proof-of-work mining system to a new and more efficient proof-of-stake algorithm. Rather than having computers solve problems to verify blocks, it will instead have people verify transactions simply by holding ETH in their wallets. It's an increasingly common mining method for new coins, but modifying an old blockchain like Ethereum to this newer concept is a lot more difficult than starting fresh.

What makes bitcoin and Ethereum different?

One of the main differences between the two super cryptocurrencies is that bitcoin is capped at a supply of 21 million. There will never be more than 21 million bitcoin, a limit it is expected to reach by 2140. Meanwhile, ETH has an unlimited supply, but the creation of new coins is very tightly controlled to keep inflation from ruining the coin's value.

Some other differences are found in the way bitcoin and Ethereum are growing over time, and in the other coins and blockchains they're working with. For example, a system called Rootstock is being developed as an attachment for the bitcoin blockchain. If it works, this attachment will bring smart contract technology to the bitcoin blockchain where needed.

Meanwhile, Ethereum has developed its own industry standard commonly called ERC20. This is like a set of measurements for cryptocurrency to allow for greater compatibility between multiple currencies.

These standards are very useful. Just like a train needs to be exactly wide enough to ride on a set of train tracks, cryptocurrencies need to have exactly the right programming to fit into wallets and be easily transferred.

By creating the ERC20 standard, coins that use the Ethereum network can start off with the right match and more easily become popular and widely used. The rest of the ecosystem, like wallets and exchanges, don't need to adapt to a new way of doing things since they're already familiar with how ERC20 works. Already, countless new ERC20 coins have forked off Ethereum, and it's been one of the main sources of new cryptocurrencies.

Cross-chain compatibility

It's important to note that there are other upcoming developments in the works that are set to make different coins more compatible. For example, the ShapeShift and Atomic Swap systems allow for more seamless exchanging of one coin for another without needing to buy or sell them through an exchange.

These, and other, "cross-chain" developments are designed to let people connect different blockchains together and transfer coins more freely between them. Bitcoin and Ethereum started off being very similar and then got very different over time. Despite their different approaches to the issue of scaling, both could be coming back to meet in the middle with similar features and easier integration with each other.

D – XRP (RIPPLE)

Symbol: *XRP*
Initial release date: *2012*
Encryption algorithm: *Ripple Protocol Consensus Algorithm (RPCA)*
Max. supply: *100 billion*
Est. total market cap ownership: *8%*

Ripple is a company building a fast money transfer network for use by its cryptocurrency, known as XRP. The Ripple network, known as RippleNet, has been accepted by several banks as a legitimate money transfer system, and the currency (XRP) offers a range of useful features. It's a bit more complicated than most cryptocurrencies, though.

The goal of Ripple is to be a global settlement network. It plans to do this by developing a platform to allow anyone to transfer money in any currency to any currency in a matter of seconds – and to do it with only a token fee. This is an ambitious goal meant to eliminate the use of older systems like Western Union or SWIFT and to greatly improve the way money is transferred across borders.

Consider this scenario: Alice and Bob need to send some money to each other. Alice uses Jamaican dollars (JMD) to conduct her business, while Bob operates in Bangladeshi taka (BDT). While it might not be evident to end users, the process behind Alice sending Bob money involves converting the JMD to a common currency like USD, then transferring the money between Alice's bank and Bob's. Finally, after this step, the USD in Bob's bank is converted back to BDT.

This incurs a lot of fees at every exchange and wastes a lot of time. The Ripple network and its XRP currency aim to fix this problem.

The alternative Ripple proposes is the use of XRP as a common currency underlying all money transfers between different currencies (USD is currently the most common currency). Not only are transaction fees much lower to convert from one currency to XRP and back through the Ripple network's blockchain, but transfers take a maximum of four seconds to execute and verify.

Quite a few global banks – over 75 as of March 2018 – have already started embracing Ripple as it saves them a lot of money in the long run by avoiding exchange fees.

What is RippleNet?

Global financial markets recognize the US$1.6 billion in savings that Ripple could create. While the price of Ripple (XRP) is inevitably the talking point within cryptocurrency circles, a closer look at its technology and how Ripple Labs, the company that created Ripple, is applying that technology is important. Ripple Labs aims to simplify cross-border payments. To do this, they are focusing on three pathways: payments processing, sending payments and source liquidity.

The three solutions Ripple Labs has created are xCurrent, which focuses mainly on the large institutional payments processing market; xRapid, which is the source of XRP liquidity; and xVia, which offers a business-to-business payments sending solution.

By looking at the stated intent of Ripple technologies, one can estimate what particular technologies are being applied in specific use case scenarios. By looking at some use cases for the existing technologies, a pattern begins to emerge showing the evolution of Ripple and how that might impact its future.

xCurrent: xCurrent is the most advanced and tested solution of Ripple Labs. It has been trialed with central banks that include the US Federal Reserve, the ECB, the Monetary Authority of Singapore and Bank Indonesia, among others. This payments processing solution is exciting and may have the largest effect on the international system of payments if it remains competitive in the field. As it is, it aims to replace the existing SWIFT system of payments processing.

xCurrent is described on Ripple's website as "Ripple's enterprise software solution that enables banks to instantly settle cross-border payments with end-to-end tracking. Using xCurrent, banks message each other in real-time to confirm payment details prior to initiating the transaction and to confirm delivery once it settles."

In 2017, xCurrent was responsible for transferring the lowly sum of US$180 between Swedish bank SEB and one of its US clients. In addition to that, the largest cross-border payments generator in the world, Singapore has been using xCurrent to power transactions. Standard Chartered of Singapore and AXIS Bank of India have been transacting local currencies with the use of xCurrent.

xRapid: The Ripple website describes xRapid as being "for payment providers and other financial institutions who want to minimize liquidity costs. Because payments into emerging markets often require pre-funded local currency accounts around the world, liquidity costs are high…"

xRapid is, in effect, powered by XRP. However, this does not help understand what xRapid actually is or what it does. With limited information, it appears as though xRapid functions as a pool of liquidity, which means a ready-made source of XRP. The idea seems to be that when a bank needs to have XRP available, it would make a currency exchange request and xRapid would make sure that the XRP is there.

From an operational perspective, xRapid's use seems to have some challenges. For example, if Standard Chartered wanted to use XRP to transfer from the Singaporean dollar to the New Zealand dollar, would Standard Chartered have to purchase XRP first or would xRapid function sort of like an overdraft account? Perhaps it's questions like these that are slowing the uptake of XRP in cross-border payments.

Another challenge for the use of xRapid is the sustained period of wild price swings XRP has experienced in its short lifespan. However, Ripple Labs has signed some important contracts for xRapid use. While xRapid does have challenges ahead, the xRapid project seems to be building steam in 2018.

xVia: On the Ripple website, xVia is described as "being for corporates, payment providers and banks who want to send payments across various networks using a standard interface. xVia›s simple API requires no software installation and enables users to seamlessly send payments globally with transparency into the payment status and with rich information, like invoices, attached."

By analyzing information on the Ripple website, it seems that xVia is the least developed solution of the three, but that is not to say that it is going to fail. Far from that, the cryptocurrency community was abuzz with speculation that eBay's public "dumping" of PayPal as a senior payments provider had something to do with Ripple.

eBay announced it would be promoting Adyen as a payments provider over the coming years. eBay joins Adyen's list of clients, which also include Uber, Netflix and Spotify among other high-volume payments senders. The exciting thing here is that the existing technology of Ripple Labs has the capacity to transfer seamlessly to Adyen.

Analyzing existing information, xVia seems to fit well with the purposes of Adyen and will capture efficiencies not yet optimized by Adyen.

Phases of implementation

Looking at the business progression, the three different financial solutions seem to be going online in three phases.

In the first phase, xCurrent has been wheeled out to central banks and major cross-border payments providers. In phase two, xRapid is being developed and shown alongside the announcements of several financial institutions agreeing to its use. Phase three appears to be quite a way off and uncertain, even if Adyen does eventually use xVia.

Being a Google Ventures-backed company, Ripple Labs is well placed to be competitive in the US market for payments processing. The way things are shaping up, RippleNet could be involved in payments processing all the way from the central bank level to the consumer base. This is still uncertain though as there is strong competition from the likes of Stellar.

The difference between Ripple and XRP

Ripple is a company; XRP is a cryptocurrency. It's a confusing distinction because saying "XRP" doesn't really roll off the tongue as smoothly saying, "I bought some Ripple." However, that phrase would be incorrect. You cannot buy some Ripple, you can only buy some XRP. It may be a case of semantics, but the distinction is imported when the situation is viewed form a wider view.

Here is a breakdown of the distinctions between the two to help you better use the two correctly when conversing in the cryptocurrency industry and community.

What is it (Ripple): A privately-owned tech company based in San Francisco, USA. Ripple also has offices in New York, London, Sydney, India, Singapore and Luxembourg. **What is it (XRP):** Independent digital asset native to the XRP Ledger. The XRP Ledger is an open-source, decentralised cryptographic ledger powered by a network of peer-to-peer servers.

What does it do (Ripple): Provides solutions designed to make it quicker, easier and cheaper to send money globally. **What does it do (XRP):** A bridge currency that acts as a cross-border payment liquidity source for banks and payment providers, facilitating transactions between different fiat currencies.

What is the relationship (Ripple): As a technology company, Ripple uses XRP and the XRP Ledger in xRapid, a product designed to provide banks and payment providers with access to on-demand liquidity. Ripple does not own or control the technology behind XRP, but it does hold 60 billion XRP (approximately 55 billion of which is locked in escrow). **What is the relationship (XRP):** XRP and the XRP Ledger are both used by Ripple, but neither can be owned by any single entity. They exist independently of any one person or business.

Who controls it (Ripple): Ripple's board, founders and employees. **Who controls it (XRP):** The users of XRP and the XRP Ledger, or anyone else in the community who contributes to XRP or the XRP Ledger.

Who uses it (Ripple): Ripple offers products for use by banks and financial institutions. **Who uses it (XRP):** Anyone can use XRP or build on the XRP Ledger.

Who owns it (Ripple): Ripple founders, investors and employees who own stock in the company. **Who owns it (XRP):** Anone can own XRP by purchasing it on an exchange.

How is XRP different from bitcoin?

The Ripple coin XRP and the Ripple Network have been built with slightly different purposes in mind, and it's worth considering whether they provide advantages over bitcoin. First, it is fast and cheap.

XRP transaction processing only takes four seconds since it's a significantly less active blockchain compared to bitcoin. This has the added bonus of cheaper transaction fees, whereas the price for bitcoin transactions has been on the rise lately as more people adopt the platform.

XRP isn't powered by mining. All of the 100 billion XRP that can be used on the platform already exist, although they're not all on the market. A few are released into the market every month to avoid flooding.

Ripple pledged to lock up 55 billion XRP in 55 different smart contracts, essentially putting billions of dollars in escrow. Each month, a contract then releases one billion XRP into the market. The primary motivator for this move was the fear that Ripple would suddenly reduce the price of the coin by releasing the billions of XRP that it's holding onto the market. The move to lock up XRP will mimic the effect of mining as seen in other currencies like bitcoin, with the goal of keeping XRP steadily growing

Now you may be wondering who powers the nodes in the network if there is no incentive for the community to donate their computational power as miners. With XRP, the banks are the nodes, and they are saving money (rather than earning it) by using its more efficient and cheaper means of transferring money between currencies.

Another key difference between bitcoin and XRP is the fact that XRP has been accepted by banks. This acceptance gives the process legitimacy and, at least from a purchaser's standpoint, can be a little more reassuring. This is not the case with bitcoin and other cryptocurrencies as they are seen as competition by the banks.

Where can you use XRP?

XRP is still a long way from being as widely accepted as bitcoin, Litecoin or Ether. It was never the goal to use Ripple as a payment method. Instead, the aim has always been to use XRP to grease the wheels in order to make fiat money transfers easier, faster and more secure. However, there are still some merchants that accept Ripple. You can find a list on the XRP forums. Transferring money with Ripple works like any other cryptocurrency:

1. **Have some XRP available in your wallet:** XRP wallets are the same as, for example, bitcoin wallets. Buy XRP on an exchange and then transfer the coins to your wallet.

2. **Scan or enter the recipient's address:** Whether they provide you with the hashed wallet address or a QR code, just follow the simple instructions on your wallet of choice and you'll be done in no time.

3. **Enter the amount and send:** The transaction should be verified in a few seconds and you're done.

Since mining is not allowed on XRP, there are only two major ways to make money from it. You can get paid in XRP or you can purchase it.

Anyone who decides to get paid in XRP will see the coin sitting in their wallets, but will also be helping the currency gain legitimacy and wider use. Ripple will benefit from any merchant accepting the XRP currency.

You can also purchase Ripple directly. While the Ripple platform might not be easily accessible to traders, anyone can find a way to buy XRP. As more and more merchants and banks adopt the platform, it's possible its price will increase, too.

What to watch out for with Ripple

As much as some people love Ripple and see it as the next generation of cryptocurrencies, there are also some who have concerns over privacy and centralization.

Privacy concerns: Cryptocurrency has always been considered the poster child of privacy and anonymity. Ripple's decision to market its platform exclusively to traditional banks has been a cause of concern for some users who continue to worry about big brother keeping an eye on their transactions.

Centralization: Ripple's platform is extremely centralized whereas most cryptocurrencies aim to be as decentralized as possible. The reason for this is that Ripple owns the vast majority of the coins available on the platform while currencies like bitcoin allow anyone to mine and acquire coins. The move to lock coins inside smart contracts was a step in the right direction to fix this issue, but every time the coins are released, they first go to Ripple to do with them as it pleases.

Competition: As a pure store of value rather than a functional token, bitcoin is arguably in competition with any other coin that's being bought and sold.

But Ripple has competition of its own to contend with. This might be one of the main challenges to its value in the future. Plus, there's also the possibility that a true global cryptocurrency could mean Ripple's ability to facilitate international fiat currency transfers is much less useful.

One of the main alternatives to Ripple is Stellar Lumens (XLM), which was also designed to facilitate international transactions. The main difference is that Stellar is designed to let people do it themselves, peer-to-peer, while Ripple is integrating with banks and existing services. You'll find a more detailed comparison of the two coins at the end of this chapter.

It's also worth noting that Ripple's extremely low transaction fees, extremely fast transfers and high scalability aren't particularly unique for newer cryptocurrencies. For example, some cryptocurrencies, such as top 50 cryptocurrency Verge, are aiming to offer completely free near-instant transactions.

What affects the price of XRP?

The hot topic in cryptocurrency markets is what is driving the price of Ripple (XRP). Some market pundits say it is all speculative trade; others say financial regulation or a lack of it drives the price of XRP; and yet others say that the underlying technology is what moves the price of XRP. Although it is hard to say that any one of these factors causes the movements in XRP, by looking at certain events surrounding all three, it is pretty clear that they all have a strong effect on the price of XRP.

Speculative trade: Speculative trade accounts for huge movements in the price of XRP. According to market information released by CoinMarketCap, the top three Korean cryptocurrency exchanges accounted for over 50% of daily trade in XRP. It may seem strange that Korean exchanges have been mentioned first, but this is important.

On January 8, 2018, US$200 million was wiped off the cryptocurrency market due to CoinMarketCap unexpectedly removing Korean exchanges from its pricing data. CoinMarketCap did not actually do anything other than show lots of people that there was a dramatic drop in cryptocurrency prices without Korean trade.

The effect on global cryptocurrency prices was enormous. On January 4, 2018, XRP hit an all-time high of US$3.84 according to CoinMarketCap. On that same day, Bithumb, the largest South Korean cryptocurrency exchange, showed XRP trading at roughly US$4.47, indicating a nearly 16.5% premium on South Korean exchanges.

That premium has pretty much disappeared. In the time since January 4, 2018, the margin between XRP on South Korean exchanges and CoinMarketCap had withered to just US$0.01 by early March. But not only that, the South Korean XRP trading price has shed a touch over US$4. Bithumb shows a trading price of US$1.16 compared to CoinMarketCap showing XRP at US$1.15 come the end of March 2018.

At present, speculative trade has the strongest effect on the price of XRP. This can be seen by the strong increases the Korean exchange markets have had on its price. That was until regulation became a barrier to entering the market.

Financial regulation: Lack of financial regulation allowed a huge speculative run on South Korean exchanges to develop. With one-third of the South Korean population holding cryptocurrency by some estimates, South Korea is widely held to be the most willing to embrace cryptocurrencies and blockchain technologies.

In response, South Korean banks have begun a regulatory squeeze. It was announced in early January 2018 that traders and exchanges were at risk of having accounts frozen if they were not compliant with the country's know-your-customer and anti-money laundering policies. That would mean that traders could face not being able to move national currencies into cryptocurrency trading accounts in South Korea.

Those changes seem to have stemmed the flow of people and money going into cryptocurrency markets.

Drops in trading volume are seeing huge XRP price falls. On January 29, 2018, XRP was at US$1.43 and had a 24-hour trading volume of US$1.53 billion. That number dropped to as low as US$826 million by the next day. On January 31, 2018, XRP had crashed to US$1.04 as sustained trading muscled it from going any lower. This shows that effective barriers to trading XRP on Korean exchanges have a negative effect on XRP prices.

In December of 2017, South Korea also banned foreigners from having trading accounts in South Korean exchanges. Of course, this was not much use since traders were allowed to make anonymous trades. Accordingly, anonymous cryptocurrency trading accounts were outlawed in January 2018.

Underlying technology: Ripple Labs specializes in remittances, which means cross-border payments. Prior to Ripple Labs, the SWIFT system of international payments was virtually without a competitor. That system is being made redundant right now. RippleNet, the patent technologies underlying XRP, transfers money almost instantly, to any city on Earth, whether that be XRP or US dollars or any other currency.

Ripple Labs technology is world class, but XRP has yet to gain the traction necessary to be a genuine form of currency. In 2017, Ripple announced some big contracts and some big testing partners, the US Federal Reserve and English Central Bank among them as well as Australia's Big Four banks. Also, Ripple Labs and European banking clientele were involved in moving hundreds of millions of US dollars across borders.

RippleNet is also being marketed well in Singapore, which is the largest remittances market on our planet. The Monetary Authority of Singapore (MAS) revealed that Ripple Labs was one of a number of blockchain companies involved when MAS conducted its blockchain experiment. Standard Chartered of Singapore and AXIS Bank of India have already been using RippleNet to send money across borders.

The trouble is that none of this is increasing the use of XRP.

At this stage, it is too risky for institutional banks to use XRP in cross-border payments. What this shows is that while the RippleNet technology is excellent, the underlying technology does not drive the price of XRP. The examples above have all been transacting in currencies other than XRP. In the United States and any other country where eBay is used, that could soon change.

As mentioned earlier, XRP's use will increase because it might soon power eBay's transactions. eBay had announced it will offer Adyen as a payments provider, where it will join major clients like Uber, Netflix and Spotify. Adyen has the capacity to integrate Ripple technology into its payments processing. If that were to happen, it would look as though XRP's adoption in payments could increase in those circumstances.

What does this means for the price of XRP?

For XRP, exchange trading and financial regulation may have short-term impacts on price, but the underlying technology is more likely to have long-term impacts on price. To the extent that speculative trading can affect XRP, financial regulation acts to restrict that. This is a simple outcome of supply and demand.

The demand for XRP on Korean exchanges was because barriers to the market were low. As barriers to the market have been introduced and strengthened, the volume of XRP trade has dropped as well as its price. Effectively, what this means is that control of XRP price falls more closely with Ripple Labs. There is evidence that suggests 91.46 billion XRP are held in the top 59 wallets and all of them hold 100 million XRP or more.

For Ripple Labs, it makes good business sense to have a stable XRP price, which allows institutional banking clients to use XRP to make cross-border payments. Even if that does not happen, the use of RippleNet seems to be increasing with Adyen being a partner. But at this stage, it is not possible to say that will drive the price of XRP.

Even if the price of XRP stabilizes, it cannot be known whether XRP will be used by its clientele. If there was one thing to share, effective regulation has curbed speculative trading and lowered the price of XRP.

What's next for Ripple?

The company behind Ripple plans to improve the lack of decentralization. By adding more trusted validator nodes, the company plans to shake off the image that it's just another central bank controlling the Ripple currency.

With that said, the future of Ripple appears to depend entirely on the adoption of the platform by banks and that's where the focus of the people behind Ripple probably needs to be. As more banks join the network, the price of XRP may continue to rise, driving more people to the coin and enticing banks to join the platform.'

More on the move to decentralization: As we've detailed earlier in this book, nodes on a blockchain network are the systems that manage its security and process transactions. They're essentially the backbone of a blockchain network. Validators are the consensus network. Their job is to independently and automatically keep their own ledger of transactions. But if one party has too much control of the validator network, they might be able to take control of the network and all the cryptocurrency in it. This is why decentralization is important. It reduces the chance of this happening.

Ripple says it's moving towards decentralization of RippleNet through protocol updates. This preliminary strategy was first announced in May 2017, and crystalized around a two-step plan in October 2017. The first step is already underway. It involves technical and infrastructure updates to lay the groundwork for a more decentralized network. Specifically, this will involve the publishing of a Unique Node List (UNL), which lays out the different nodes on the Ripple network. If a node doesn't appear on this list, it's not considered legitimate.

The second step involves managed decentralization in the form of adding independent validators to the network. For every two independent validators added to the UNL, one Ripple-operated validator will be removed. This should have the effect of creating a much more diverse and resilient Ripple network.

"The end state will be a network with a varied set of validators, operated by multiple entities from different locations, all sharing one goal: the long term health and stability of the XRP Ledger," stated Ripple n February 2018. "Maintaining our momentum towards further decentralization is critical for XRP Ledger to reach its full potential."

The Ripple papers: This new approach was also accompanied by the release of peer-reviewed academic papers. Developers for other blockchain systems, such as those using bitcoin and Ethereum, have frequently released these in an effort to document their tests and forward understanding of the field as a whole, but Ripple hadn't dipped its toes into these waters before.

The two papers are each related to one of the upgrade phases. The first is Analysis of the XRP Ledger Consensus Protocol, which provides formal mathematical proof of ongoing efficacy of the Ripple network. The follow-up is Cobalt: BFT Governance in Open Networks, which describes the second phase efforts to implement a more diverse range of validators to improve network security.

"This is the first time we're releasing peer-reviewed academic papers. Obviously, it opens the door for future research. After this, I expect you'll hear much more about us interacting with academia," said Ripple CTO Stefan Thomas of their release.

A matter of security: One of the main goals of these decentralizing efforts is to uphold network security. Centralization can take various forms, and many cryptocurrencies have different reasons for opposing specific types of centralization. In Ripple's case, it's specifically pursuing greater decentralization of validators in order to better secure the network against outside attack.

"What we're trying to do here is add some defenses against unlikely attack scenarios. Basically, it says you can't completely manipulate the entire network," Thomas explained.

Even without these systems, you'd still need a lot of resources to disrupt the existing Ripple network, with Thomas saying the attacks would only be viable when carried out by a state actor, rather than an individual or smaller organization. It might have sounded a bit paranoid a few years ago, but as cryptocurrencies move into the mainstream, and Ripple is taken up by national central banks, it might be a critical part of development.

Ripple is responding to market needs. There is decentralization in the form of validator diversity, and also transparency in the form of the Ripple papers, which might both be necessary steps for Ripple to grow.

As an added bonus, it might also help give regulators around the world more clarity and unity on Ripple's exact capabilities, which may help pave the way to quicker adoption of XRP as a settlement system.

If you're thinking of buying Ripple, you can see a comparison of exchanges that trade in the token on the finder website.

E – STELLAR LUMENS

Symbol: *XLM*
Initial release date: *2014*
Encryption algorithm: *Stellar Consensus Protocol*
Max. supply: *100 billion*
Est. total market cap ownership: *1.5%*

Now would seem like a good time to talk about Stellar Lumens. As mentioned at the end of the last chapter, Stellar is a bi-product of Ripple that essentially aims to be more fully decentralized, as opposed to operating primarily through banks.

Stellar was actually a fork of Ripple way back in 2014; however, they no longer share a common code base. It still works in a very similar way to Ripple and allows for instant transactions across borders throughout the world. However, the biggest difference is that Ripple is fairly centralized since Ripple itself determines who may act as a transaction validator on their network.

Stellar, on the other hand, runs an open ledger, which anyone can access, open and join. The centralized nature of Ripple is something that turns crypto purists off since they believe that the biggest advantage of cryptocurrencies is that they are decentralized. Stellar promises a lot of what Ripple can do but sticks to that core decentralized belief.

Unlike Ripple, which is focused mainly on big banks and institutions, Stellar wants to solve issues in developing markets around managing money and transactions, particularly across different countries. Stellar Lumens already has live payments between Europe and the Philippines and is looking to add Africa and the Middle East throughout 2018.

If you look at Ripple's growth over the past couple of months, it becomes pretty clear that most of it was due to the fact that it had an awesome PR run thanks to some great deals it made in Asia and in the USA with American Express.

Stellar, on the other hand, has barely had a peep come out about it, with the pumping of the price mostly coming from its community. If it begins to appear more in the general public, its potential to grow may increase, particularly if a major exchange such as Coinbase were to pick it up.

How does Stellar work?

Stellar lets anyone send, receive or trade any kind of currency, whether fiat or crypto, with anyone else in the world almost immediately and at practically no cost. Lumens (XLM) is the name of the cryptocurrency token, while Stellar is the name of the network as a whole.

Stellar is essentially a matchmaker for various currencies and facilitates worldwide transfers and exchanges.

It focuses on simplicity and scalability as well as on functionality to help move money in remote areas at lower costs. There are three different ways you can do this.

- **Direct exchange:** You can make direct currency exchanges. For example, if one person wants to trade USD for AUD and another person wants to trade AUD for USD, it can match them and then automatically carry out the exchange for the two requested amounts.

- **Exchange via XLM:** Stellar can use XLM as an intermediary currency where the amounts don't add up or there isn't a direct exchange available. It simultaneously looks for buy and sell offers for XLM and the needed currencies. Once it finds a good offer, it then handles the exchange.

- **Chain of conversions:** If no other options are available, Stellar will try to handle any currency by finding a chain of conversions, such as AUD to BTC to EUR to USD.

The Stellar network is doing all of the above at the same time. When you make a transfer, it will aim to provide the best possible rates every single transaction. If you simply want to send or receive money rather than make an exchange, it can do that by directly connecting individual entities.

When using the Stellar network, you'll typically use the ledger and anchors. The ledger is a central record of every account on the network and the currencies it holds. This information is needed to make transfers around the network effective. The anchors are trusted entities on the network that hold the currencies being transferred. An anchor might be anything from a bank to a person in a remote village who takes the money online and then hands the recipient the cash.

Security features

One of the notable features of Stellar is its ability to freeze transfers. For example, you can freeze a transfer if you've mistakenly entered the wrong wallet address. This is unlike the irreversible transfers of most other cryptocurrencies. Once transfers are frozen, the funds are unable to be used by the recipient.

Also, while all transactions on the network are public by default, transactions can be made private and confidential through the use of third-party plugins. And like other blockchain systems, the Stellar network is a decentralized application run on computers all around the world. This makes it almost entirely failsafe.

If the non-profit Stellar organization disappeared, its network would keep going. It's worth noting that in order to use the Stellar network, you need to have at least 20 XLM coins. This ensures some vested interest in the ecosystem by those who use it.

What to consider when buying Lumens

The initial supply of Stellar Lumens was set at around 100 billion XLM, of which around 18 billion are in circulation. It's worth considering that Stellar has built inflation into its system in the form of members getting gifted small amounts of free XLM over time. A fraction of the Lumens collected with each operation goes towards this inflation, along with other XLM released into circulation.

It's also worth remembering that Stellar is a non-profit organization aimed at creating a more inclusive world economy for everyone. A high price for Lumens might undermine that goal, prevent people from listing their XLM on the ledger to facilitate exchanges and drive up the average cost of transfers, so there's a real incentive to keep prices in check. It's safe to say XLM prices won't ever skyrocket in value the way bitcoin has.

However, Stellar has also formed partnerships with major companies like IBM and specifically aims to offer low cost, easy business money transfers. It looks like many organizations are aiming to use Stellar for their money transfer needs and wider use is likely to see prices climb over time.

Buying Lumens also gives users the means to more easily interact with a range of fiat currencies. Forex enthusiasts, frequent travelers or anyone else who can benefit from cheap, quick and easy access to a variety of fiat currencies might get their money's worth from buying Lumens even if the price doesn't increase.

What is the Stellar Decentralized Exchange (SDEX)?

A decentralized exchange is a distributed marketplace. Users around the world hold their own funds and then trade them directly with each other as needed. The funds don't pass through the exchange and there's no intermediary. Decentralized exchanges are basically matchmaking services for users and vehicles for useful features and user interfaces.

The Stellar Decentralized Exchange (SDEX), also known as Stellarport, is different to most decentralized exchanges, such as those that run on the Ethereum ecosystem, because there's only one "official" decentralized exchange that holds user listings. But it can be accessed in different ways. This helps combine some of the benefits of a central trading system (high volume, deep liquidity, many options, etc.) with the benefits of a decentralized system (cost-effectiveness, security and reliability).

Think of it as a magical online bazaar that's everywhere and nowhere, with different doors that lead to it. Stellarport is a brand new door, but the marketplace itself already existed. More doors mean more people might be buying and selling there.

This exchange also includes its own wallet system for users, which seems to have been designed with an emphasis on user-friendliness and accessibility. The landing page gives users only three options.

Stellar's 2018 roadmap suggests a focus on its decentralized exchange, and systems like Stellarport could help the ecosystem grow. The lack of a pleasing trading interface was previously regarded as one of Stellar's bugbears. StellarTerm came along and presented a nicer option than the bare bones original, and now Stellarport has entered with an alternative that some people might prefer. More options for a wider range of users always seem like a good thing.

The trade volumes of Stellar (XLM) and other coins available on Stellarport - like Mobius (MOBI) and Smartlands (SLT) - all seem to have jumped since Stellarport's launch, according to CoinMarketCap, especially against the backdrop of a relatively stagnant cryptocurrency market. This might suggest that a lot of people are trying Stellarport.

Plus, at this stage it might be healthier for cryptos to detach themselves from bitcoin's market impacts. The growing Stellar model of a "central" decentralized exchange might suggest an effective path.

More on Stellarport

The Stellar Lumens Decentralized Exchange, Stellarport, is now up and running. The exchange has been active for a while now and can be accessed in various ways (such as the StellarTerm interface), but Stellarport might be one of the more convenient all-in-one options. This is because it not only allows you to buy and sell XLM without the fees of a centralized exchange, but also because it offers a Stellar wallet.

As of March 2018, the bulk of Stellar trading looks like XLM:MOBI pairs (trading Stellar for Mobius), but all the native Stellar ecosystem tokens are present, including Smartlands (SLT) and SureRemit (RMT), as well as fiat currencies in the form of CNY (Chinese Yuan Renminbi). Stellar ecosystem tokens refer to cryptocurrencies that have forked off Stellar or otherwise use its network.

Note: Stellarport is not part of the Stellar Foundation. It's essentially a separate company that's decided to build on the Stellar system. This is par for course with cryptocurrencies, but worth noting anyway.

What's next for Stellar?

When Stellar Lumens dropped its 2018 roadmap on January 25, 2018, the main highlight was its goal of creating a much wider Stellar ecosystem over the year through increased support for ICOs and other improvements.

There were two main steps taking the technology towards that goal. The first step involved upgrades to the SDEX, including better technical documentation, implementation walkthroughs and general brand communication. The second step involved the implementation of the Lightning Network, including improved node reliability and self-sufficiency, and decreased overheads to help further decentralize the network.

How SDEX will help ICOs: "In 2018, we will putting very significant energy into bringing a wider variety of financial instruments on to the network," reads the Stellar roadmap. "SDEX will be the exchange of first resort for all Stellar tokens, and we foresee a future where, say, carbon credits, oil futures, and even the latest digital asset are all traded together - cheaply and quickly. The exchange will also promote our vision of moving more real-world assets on the blockchain."

According to the roadmap, the SDEX will be able to offer day-one trading for any Stellar ICO token. Getting a listing on a major exchange on day one is a competitive advantage for a new coin. That kind of listing on a fiat exchange such as the SDEX could also promote unusually quick uptake of a new coin post-ICO. It means potential buyers don't necessarily have to part with other crypto assets to buy in, and that cryptocurrency newcomers can also get involved right away.

Other SDEX improvements promised in the roadmap include the following:

- Atomic pathfinding to discover the cheapest rates between any two assets.

- Very low trading fees.

- End-user control of secret keys.

- More and better anchors and market makers.

According to the roadmap, "the Exchange also promotes our vision of moving more real-world assets on the blockchain. ICOs are already coming to Stellar because we're cheap, scalable, and fast."

Lightning Network: "We've noted the market demand for more private channel transactions on Stellar," continued the roadmap, "and we will integrate Lightning in 2018... Lightning will have a huge positive effect on Stellar's long-term scalability and security."

Stellar has already taken concrete steps towards the implementation of Lightning sometime in 2018, in the form of a collaboration with Stellar advisor and bitcoin developer Jeremy Rubin. Sticking Lightning inside Stellar's already snappy (compared to many) network might solve potential scaling problems for the foreseeable future.

The introduction of private transaction channels may also be especially significant in line with the stated goals of the SDEX (trading of a wide variety of financial instruments). Moving forward, the Stellar roadmap outlines distinct benefits for ICOs, a focus on scaling and ground-up integration of a high quality decentralized exchange.

To some, this roadmap might suggest that Stellar is aiming to become one of the world's key future networks.

Possible roadblocks for Stellar Lumens

There are two potentially big roadblocks stopping Stellar from reaching bitcoin levels of growth. First, it relies too heavily on bitcoin and Ethereum, with most exchanges only allowing you to trade Stellar by selling off your other digital currencies. It needs to develop a closer link to the US dollar because if bitcoin continues its slump and XLM doesn't grow fast enough, it could see itself get dragged down with bitcoin.

Second, is its biggest competitor Ripple. Stellar Lumens is a non-profit foundation, and Ripple is a for-profit organization with a big budget behind it to push marketing and major global deals. Stellar is focusing more on the underdeveloped markets, and it will need to hope that it reaches and wins that segment before Ripple gets there.

As for price, if it gets picked up by a major broker such as Coinbase and becomes easier to trade for USD, its price could increase.

If you're thinking of buying Stellar Lumens, you can see a comparison of exchanges that trade in the token on the finder website.

F – XRP (RIPPLE) VS. LUMENS (XLM)

We mentioned through the last chapter that another cryptocurrency, Stellar Lumens, is looking to do something very similar to Ripple with its technology. So let's compare them in greater detail. As a broad overview, Ripple was created in an attempt to solve international payments and to bring lower costs and faster transfers. Then Stellar was created in an attempt to solve Ripple.

Stellar was initially based on Ripple's system and had the aim of redesigning the global economy for more inclusiveness. But citing the complexity of the system, Stellar later redesigned itself with a brand new system of its own. Both facilitate international payments, but do so in very different ways.

How Ripple works: Banks and multinational corporations use XRP to make international payments. This is done by transferring the XRP token through the Ripple network. The end result is liquidity on demand.

How Stellar works: Stellar lets individuals trade money directly with each other, using Lumens (XLM) as a medium and "anchors" to handle the fiat currency aspects.

For example, let's say Jim wants to send money from an Australian bank account to a German bank account, converting it to euros along the way. He wants to do it at the best rates possible.

With traditional money transfers

The money will be bumped between several banks on the way. It will frequently be converted from AUD to USD to EUR on the way. The entire process takes three to five days, incurs fees from each bank on the journey and loses Jim money on all the exchange rates.

With XRP: Jim could buy XRP himself and send it to a wallet overseas, but he doesn't want to. Fortunately, his bank uses XRP. He makes a money transfer as usual. His bank sends XRP directly to the bank of the recipient account. The payment is made at whatever exchange rates and fees the bank chooses to charge for this service. If Jim is lucky, the bank has passed some savings onto him. The transaction occurs in a matter of minutes.

With Stellar: Jim signs onto the Stellar platform and sends money through it. It makes the transfer automatically. First, it converts the AUD to euros, and then it uses an anchor to transfer the euros to the recipient account. An anchor is a Stellar partner that's entrusted with actually transferring the funds. These are usually money transfer companies. Jim can choose his own anchor and shop around for the one he wants.

There are a few different ways Jim's AUD might be converted into euros.

- **Peer to peer:** It looks for people who want to trade euros for AUD and then picks the best prices.

- **Via XLM:** Lumens (XLM) are used to fill the gaps or make up the entire transfer if needed. For example, the Stellar platform might sell Lumens for euros through an existing order on the official Stellar exchange.

- **Chain of conversions:** The platform can automatically perform a chain of conversions, such as AUD > NZD > CNY > USD > EUR if that's what it takes.

Between these options, which are carried out automatically, and with XLM to fill in the gaps and grease the wheels, people can make efficient peer-to-peer money transfers or simply convert currency for their own purposes.

Neither is inherently better or worse than the other and despite having the same functions, each was built for different purposes. XRP allows multinational companies and banks to quickly make cost-effective international transfers and currency conversions, plus access a range of extra features. Ripple is a privately owned blockchain company that provides its services to other companies. Stellar allows individuals to make more cost-effective money transfers and currency transfers. Stellar itself is a non-profit organization with the goal of enabling a more inclusive global payment system.

When deciding which crypto to hold, you will need to take into account a number of considerations. For example, both XRP and XLM saw dramatic price increases at the end of 2017 and drops at the start of 2018, and their values have tended to mirror each other. This may suggest that many people are holding both rather than picking just one or the other.

Another consideration is the fact that Ripple has partnered with a lot of high-profile banks, so there's a lot of money behind it from the existing financial ecosystem. It also offers a range of features that Stellar can't match, including smart contract functionality. On the other hand, you will also need to take into account the possibility of Stellar getting enough users and anchors that it could feasibly let people exchange currencies seamlessly and much cheaper than with XRP.

Also, technology has increasingly moved towards decentralization, and you will need to decide if Stellar is ahead of Ripple in that respect and if it matters.

G – BITCOIN CASH

Symbol: *BCH*
Initial release date: *August 1, 2017*
Encryption algorithm: *SHA-256*
Max. supply: *21 million*
Est. total market cap ownership: *5%*

Bitcoin Cash has rapidly become one of the most valuable cryptocurrencies in the world. In an effort to improve the efficiency of transactions, Bitcoin Cash broke off from the original bitcoin network on August 1, 2017. Bitcoin Cash aims to take bitcoin in a new direction geared towards faster transaction speeds and lower fees.

What is Bitcoin Cash?

Originally built upon the famed bitcoin model, the digital currency Bitcoin Cash has the following characteristics:

- **Decentralized:** The network is spread out across many different computers all over the world.

- **Peer-to-Peer:** Person A can send Bitcoin Cash directly to Person B from anywhere in the world without needing an intermediary, like a bank.

- **Secure:** Bitcoin Cash uses strong encryption algorithms to prevent hacking, fraud and cyber-attacks.

- **Open:** The history of all Bitcoin Cash transactions is logged on a publicly accessible blockchain that can be viewed and verified by anyone.

Bitcoin Cash was created as a result of diverging viewpoints within the bitcoin community about how to scale the network. As more people began to use bitcoin, the network struggled to keep up with the volume of transactions. As a result, many bitcoin users were waiting hours, sometimes days, before seeing their transactions go through.

There was a lot of debate around the community on how to solve this problem and that led to a split between two groups with opposing viewpoints: those in favor of increasing the size of the blocks in the blockchain versus those in favor of restructuring the way data was stored in the existing blocks.

The group within the bitcoin community that wanted to increase the size of the blocks on the bitcoin blockchain consisted primarily of bitcoin miners. This group could not get enough support from the larger bitcoin community to form the consensus needed to move bitcoin in this direction. As a result, this group split off (or "hard forked") from the original bitcoin blockchain and formed Bitcoin Cash as a new currency.

Bitcoin Cash recognizes the same blockchain as bitcoin up until the time of the fork, August 1, 2017. After the fork, Bitcoin Cash transactions started to be recorded on a new blockchain, specific to Bitcoin Cash, while bitcoin continued to maintain the original bitcoin blockchain.

What does Bitcoin Cash do differently?

The biggest difference between bitcoin and Bitcoin Cash has to do with the size of the blocks on the blockchain. By increasing block size from bitcoin's 1MB up to 8MB, Bitcoin Cash allows many more transactions to be processed in one block. The idea is to process larger transaction volumes faster and for lower fees.

Another significant difference between the two currencies is that the level of difficulty involved in mining Bitcoin Cash varies depending on how many miners are active on the network. Many bitcoin miners have migrated over to Bitcoin Cash for this reason because it allows them to generate larger profits at a faster rate than mining bitcoin.

Where can I use Bitcoin Cash as payment?

Many cryptocurrency exchanges have taken steps to integrate Bitcoin Cash, and it's possible that merchants will begin to follow suit as the currency continues to grow. For those looking to use cryptocurrency to buy goods and services, Bitcoin Cash is not currently accepted by most vendors, including many of those that do accept bitcoin.

How to get Bitcoin Cash

There are a few ways to get your hands on some BCH. In fact, you might already have some.

If you owned bitcoin before the August 1 fork, you might already have Bitcoin Cash. Any bitcoin holdings you had prior to the split, unless they were kept on an exchange, can also be claimed as Bitcoin Cash. The same private keys associated with your bitcoin wallet can be used to access equal holdings in Bitcoin Cash.

Buy from an exchange. Initially, many of the most prominent exchanges in the US were hesitant to support Bitcoin Cash. However, due to an increase in value and consumer demand, more and more exchanges are beginning to open their doors to this new currency.

Mine it. Bitcoin Cash has received a lot of support from miners, many of whom have switched over from mining bitcoin. The opportunity to earn generous amounts of BCH through mining is an incentive for more people to participate in the network.

What should I consider before buying Bitcoin Cash?

Cryptocurrencies are notoriously volatile, and it's impossible to say for certain whether the value of Bitcoin Cash will go up or down. Since its initial release, BCH has grown to become one of the most valuable cryptocurrencies in the world, but it has also seen major price fluctuations from one day to the next.

From a trader perspective, the stability of Bitcoin Cash needs to be reviewed. Many skeptics believe that it will not be able to replace bitcoin as the leader in this space and may not survive in the long term. On the other hand, supporters of BCH believe it offers an improvement over bitcoin and will therefore gain value in the long term and ultimately overtake its predecessor.

Ultimately, Bitcoin Cash is still very new, and it has seen major price variations in its early days. There's ongoing debate about the real value of Bitcoin Cash, how much support it has and whether its solution to bitcoin's scaling problem is ultimately a success. Plus, as bitcoin moves to implement its own solutions to the scaling issue, we will likely get a much clearer picture of how these two competing currencies will develop into the future.

Bitcoin vs. Bitcoin Cash

Bitcoin Cash is the result of a bitcoin fork, so it's extremely similar in many ways to bitcoin. However, Bitcoin Cash has a few technical differences that make a big impact.

Bitcoin Cash's larger block size is good news in that it helps process transactions a lot faster, but it also means a full node takes up a lot more data storage space. A full node is required to mine on the blockchain. It includes a copy of the entire transaction history for the whole blockchain. So as you can imagine, a larger block size comes with higher hardware and data storage costs.

One of the main arguments against a larger block size is that it leads to increased centralization of a coin, and that the higher hardware costs mean only large mining groups will be able to profitably work on the blockchain.

Other differences are in the mining algorithm. At its inception, Bitcoin Cash had an easier mining algorithm. Mining difficulty refers to how quickly a block can be discovered and attached to the blockchain. To solve a block, the miner needs to spend processing power on solving a complex math problem. By making the problem easier, blocks can be mined faster. By making it harder, blocks are mined slower.

On the bitcoin and Bitcoin Cash blockchains, fast and easy blocks are good for transaction times, but not necessarily good for the currency in the long run. This is because miners are rewarded with newly minted coins for solving these problems and finding new blocks. If it's too easy, the currency faces too-high inflation rates and gets devalued. Although it's worth noting that both BTC and BCH will get considerably more difficult to mine as they get closer to their 21 million coin limit.

For more on bitcoin mining, read the guide on the finder website.

An easier mining algorithm was deemed to be necessary for BCH to keep a competitive edge against the more valuable bitcoin. This is because it would act to attract the miners needed to run the network.

Soon this had the unintended side effect of miners dipping in and out of BCH based on whether it was profitable at the time, leading to extremely unpredictable block times. Sometimes blocks would be hours apart (for very slow transactions), and sometimes they would come along within just a few seconds of each other (for very fast transactions, but rapid inflation).

In response, BCH introduced a dynamic mining algorithm which would get easier or more difficult as needed. This helped introduce some more consistency to the BCH blockchain and keep more miners working on it.

So which is better?

Each is good at a different thing. The high fees and slow transaction times of the original bitcoin are a deliberate, but somewhat unfortunate, design choice. It's intended to keep the coin rare, challenging and valuable. The bitcoin community and developers are banking on bitcoin being a "store of value" for cryptocurrency as a whole, just like gold used to underpin the US dollar and other fiat currencies. No one actually uses gold as a currency, but it still offers liquidity and value. The idea is that bitcoin could be digital gold.

Bitcoin Cash was deliberately split away from bitcoin by a team who thought high fees and slow transactions would eventually destroy bitcoin. It was deliberately designed to essentially be bitcoin, except easier to send, receive and transact with. Hence the "cash" part of its name. It was designed to be the spending money next to bitcoin's gold.

Will Bitcoin Cash overtake bitcoin?

No one can say for sure, but you'll find a lot of strong opinions in both directions. However, bitcoin's transaction functionality seems to be the main issue. For example, the first major Bitcoin Cash growth spurt came at the start of November 2017, following the news that the bitcoin B2X hard fork was cancelled.

This hard fork was intended to solve some of bitcoin's frustrating transaction problems. When it was called off, people argued that the growth came from users trading their BTC for BCH. The second major growth spurt came around the end of December 2017, when the bitcoin mempool, the number of unverified transactions, had been clogged up for the better part of a month, and there was growing dissatisfaction with bitcoin's yet-to-be-released Lightning Network.

You will need to decide whether bitcoin's transaction functionality will continue to affect Bitcoin Cash's growth as well as consider what will happen if bitcoin ever solves these problems in the future.

If you're thinking of buying Bitcoin Cash, you can see a comparison of exchanges that trade in the token on the finder website.

H – LITECOIN

Symbol: *LTC*
Initial release date: *October 7, 2011*
Encryption algorithm: *Scrypt*
Max. supply: *84 million*
Est. total market cap ownership: *3%*

Having started from very modest origins and demonstrating only subtle technical improvements over bitcoin, Litecoin (LTC) has grown to become one of the top cryptos by market cap. It is now often characterized as the silver to bitcoin's gold, but there's far more to the currency's growth than meets the eye.

Released on October 7, 2011 by former Google employee Charlie Lee, Litecoin (LTC) is an open source, peer-to-peer cryptocurrency – that is a digital currency operating independently of any country's central bank. While similar to bitcoin in many ways, Litecoin has also incorporated several features (such as Segregated Witness), which they describe as improvements to help reduce bottlenecks in the network and to increase the speed with which transactions are carried out.

Litecoin has experienced significant growth since its inception, reaching a $1 billion market cap in November 2013, and over four times that much by 2017.

How is Litecoin different from bitcoin?

While there are a lot of similarities between Litecoin and its more widely-accepted competitor, bitcoin, Litecoin states that it has a few distinct advantages when it comes to mining, transaction verification speed and security:

- **Higher volume of transactions:** In May 2017, Litecoin became the first cryptocurrency to adopt Segregated Witness (or SegWit, for short). The system splits every transaction into two segments, removing the signature (the "witness" part) from the original data. This makes the processing and verification of every transaction faster and is one of the key advantages of Litecoin over bitcoin. It reduced the time for confirmation of payment from 10 minutes (for bitcoin) to 2.5 minutes (for Litecoin).

- **More secure:** This faster processing time also helps maintain a secure environment by reducing the chance of double-spending attacks. This is a hack in which the attacker spends the same money twice for two different transactions.

- **Larger coin limit:** While bitcoin has a maximum coin limit of 21 million coins, Litecoin has an upper limit of 84 million coins.

- **Harder to mine:** This might not be seen as an advantage when first glanced, but because Litecoin uses scrypt hashing (instead of SHA-256), mining cannot be accelerated by using parallel processors as can be done when bitcoin mining. This has created a much more level playing field as opposed to the race that bitcoin mining has become.

Cryptocurrencies that allow mining of coins all use a particular hashing algorithm. The algorithm both protects the transactions and the data on the network from tampering and allows miners to collect coins by cracking the hashing and verifying the transactions themselves. The most common algorithm is SHA-256 (used in bitcoin and all its forked coins), but some currencies like Litecoin use scrypt (read: ess-crypt) instead.

You can use Litecoin nearly anywhere you can use bitcoin. Since its release, it did become the second largest cryptocurrency after bitcoin, and merchants have been quick to adopt it. The Litecoin website has an always-growing list of services, merchants and providers that accept Litecoin, ranging from financial consulting services to beauty merchants.

What to watch out for

Not unlike its bigger sibling, Litecoin has its disadvantages. Here are a few of the cryptocurrency's shortcomings:

- **Not as widely accepted:** Litecoin is still growing and while its acceptance has become more and more common over the past year, bitcoin is still the most commonly recognized cryptocurrency.

- **Not different enough:** Many consider Litecoin's technical improvements too subtle and this might hinder Litecoin's growth. Faster transaction times and more difficulty in mining might be good enough reasons for specific use cases, but in the grand scheme of things, many are of the opinion that it does not differentiate itself from bitcoin enough to sustain long-term growth.

If Litecoin's market cap continues to grow, more businesses may begin to adopt it, either alongside bitcoin or as a complete replacement. Additionally, a lot of work is being carried out on upgrading the network Litecoin runs on, which will improve the speed at which transactions are verified even further and will, more importantly, allow atomic swaps.

With Litecoin joining the Lightning Network, users will soon be able to participate in what is known as atomic cross-chain trading or atomic swaps for short. Imagine Alice needs to pay Bob. Without atomic swaps, if Bob has a bitcoin wallet and Alice only has Litecoin, she would need to first exchange her Litecoin into bitcoin, open a bitcoin wallet, then pay Bob in bitcoin. This is clumsy and has been a major hindrance to the acceptance of altcoins over bitcoin.

It's part of a promising roadmap for the coin, which also includes the arrival of new Litecoin ATMs and eventually (hopefully) the LitePay platform.

What's happening with LitePay?

LitePay is a project created by the Litecoin Foundation, one of the primary teams behind the coin. LitePay is a payment platform and was on track for its planned February 2018 launch. LitePay aimed to bridge the gap between Litecoin and fiat currency. The platform would have made it easier for businesses to accept Litecoin as payment, settle Litecoin payments directly with banks and manage Litecoin finances all in one place through the open-source LitePay mobile and desktop wallet.

It also planned to create a LitePay card, to let users load dollars into their Litecoin wallet without any fees. More importantly, it allow will allow you to use it at ATMs, merchants and anywhere else VISA cards are accepted.

Of course, Litecoin wasn't the first cryptocurrency to attempt to bridge the gap between fiat and crypto. Throughout 2017, bitcoin saw growing acceptance as a payment system, with more merchants accepting bitcoin, bitcoin debit cards and various systems to make it easier to convert fiat currencies to bitcoin and spend it on demand. On the finder website we even have a map of ATMs and shops that accept bitcoin in Australia.

However, these plans were constrained by bitcoin's high transaction fees and network congestion, and bitcoin actually became a less widely-accepted payment method the more popular it got. A lot of platforms aim to enable seamless conversions between bitcoin and fiat currency on demand, but network issues mean they're still largely untested and unable to proceed until the bitcoin Lightning Network upgrades.

Litecoin hoped to address these issues through its quicker and cheaper transactions.

Sadly, the LitePay launch was postponed indefinitely in late February 2018. Recipients on the LitePay mailing list received the news that the intended launch of LitePay is "imprudent." The mass communication email stressed that the postponement was "due to recent hostile actions by card issuers towards crypto companies." This appeared to be a direct reference to the fact that numerous major banks prohibiting the purchase of cryptocurrencies by way of credit cards.

The last-minute announcement came amid general confusion in the market surrounding its release. Despite the market being well aware of the financial industry's reluctance to process credit card cryptocurrency purchases, LitePay did not seem to consider making the announcement until the day of the intended launch.

Instead of an imminent launch, the LitePay team has stated that merchant registration for the receipt of money in Litecoin (LTC) will be completed. Markets are sure to find it difficult to take away significant amounts of confidence from a heavily watered down delivery of a much-anticipated product.

In the context of the broader cryptocurrency community, it was hoped the launch would be successful. Had LitePay successfully launched a cryptocurrency payments system, it would have been a big step in the direction of crypto replacing traditional fiat currencies.

Having shown itself to be a fizzer, a new LitePay launch date will need to be announced in the future, and no indication has been given as to when that might be as of March 2018.

In truth, LitePay has always had its skeptics. Even prior to the failed launch, questions had overshadowed the project's management. LTC founder and former Google programmer Charlie Lee announced on social media that LitePay was not a project under the supervision of the Litecoin community. That admission by Lee severely damaged LitePay's credibility even though Lee admitted to having contact with the project.

LTC itself has benefitted from the initial announcement of the LTC payments interface. In the days after Lee's tweet, the price of LTC was at US$144.66. Only hours before the news hit markets about the failed launch, LTC was at US$233.15 according to CoinMarketCap. Following the news, LTC dropped 5.2%. What is more telling is that LTC's value against bitcoin weakened sharply over the few hours after the failed launch came to light, dropping 8.99% in value against BTC.

Just as the markets have eagerly been watching the intended launch of LitePay, they will also watch the reaction to the news as speculation over the value of LTC becomes an important factor in the interim.

Litecoin price prediction

Some proponents of LTC believe it will continue to increase in value. They point out that it's like a "quarter-sized" version of bitcoin. They argue that it is more functional, but that its price is much less than a quarter of bitcoin's. The assumption among some buyers is that even if Litecoin prices peak at a quarter of bitcoin's, it can still be very worthwhile.

Towards Christmas time 2017, about two-thirds of all the Litecoin that will ever exist were already in circulation, and it can be assumed that mining will get increasingly difficult as it approaches the supply limit. This makes it more likely that the popularity of Litecoin will result in increased demand, and if demand exceeds supply in the future, that could naturally drive the prices up.

It's also worth noting that Litecoin has tended to be ahead of its time. It was the first of the top five cryptocurrencies (as viewed by market cap) to adopt the features of Segregated Witness (SegWit), which has since become standard among bitcoin and other altcoins. This ongoing development might bode well for its future popularity as it could prevent other altcoins from overtaking it later. However, like all cryptocurrencies, nothing about Litecoin can be taken for granted.

For detailed comparisons on Litecoin exchanges and wallets, visit the Litecoin hub page over on the finder website.

What is Litecoin Cash?

If you explore Litecoin, you will also come across Litecoin Cash (LCC). Litecoin Cash was founded in December 2017 by a team with no ties to the original Litecoin project. It's a hard fork off the Litecoin blockchain that uses bitcoin's SHA-256 algorithm for mining purposes to create new tokens, allowing crypto miners with old technology to put their hardware to good use again. Mining difficulty is also recalculated every block, using Evan Duffield›s DarkGravity V3 algorithm that was popularized by the cryptocurrency Dash.

But what's the purpose of this new cryptocurrency? The official Litecoin Cash answer to this question is that "There is no fast, cheap SHA256 coin with good difficulty adjustment. SHA256 miners have little practical choice of hashpower destination, and if they do mine blocks they're being paid in a currency with ten minute block times.

"We believe we can offer an excellent SHA-256 coin for general usage. We love Litecoin, and wanted to give something to the brave community that have stayed with us. With everyone else too busy forking Bitcoin, we decided that the Litecoin blockchain was a perfect means of initial distribution for our coin."

The team behind Litecoin Cash also claims that it will offer 90% cheaper transactions than Litecoin, and that the target block time of two and a half minutes provides four times the transaction bandwidth of bitcoin.

It's also attracted a lot of controversy in the Litecoin community, with Litecoin creator Charlie Lee calling the fork a scam.

However, it's not a direct copy of Litecoin. It uses the SHA-256 mining algorithm which lets people use now-obsolete bitcoin mining equipment to mine Litecoin Cash. This might be a fairly useless function for everyone except owners of said mining equipment, and in that respect it might looks like LCC was only created to make a quick buck, mostly through popping value into existence through an airdrop of 10 Litecoin Cash tokens for every 1 Litecoin token a user held at the time of the fork.

Is Litecoin Cash a scam?

It might be considered a scam in the same way Bitcoin Cash (BCH) and Bitcoin Gold (BTG), and to a certain extent bitcoin and Litecoin, are arguably scams. BCH and BTG are now the fourth and twentieth largest coins by market cap respectively as of March 2018, with a market over $25 billion between them, and over $800 million in 24-hour trade volume.

The bitcoin core community was also strongly opposed to the BCH and BTG forks, despite benefiting greatly from the anticipatory price rises and subsequent value of the airdrops. A similar effect was seen with Litecoin Cash. Litecoin prices rose considerably in the days leading up to the fork, even as LTC users complained about the fork. Now that it's forked, they're complaining about receiving the free LCC airdrop.

Is LCC is a scam? No. It's upfront and honest about only really existing to make a quick buck, the same way many other cryptocurrencies are. But it doesn't matter. Anything can have value if enough people believe in it. That's how money works. And with the potential to put their old mining gear to use, enough people might have enough incentive to give LCC value by believing in it hard enough.

If you're thinking of buying Litecoin, you can see a comparison of exchanges that trade in the token on the finder website.

I – CARDANO

Symbol: *ADA*
Initial release date: *September 29, 2017*
Encryption algorithm: *Ouroboros*
Max. supply: *45 billion*
Est. total market cap ownership: *1.4%*

Cardano is being built from the ground up and aims to be the most practical and effective cryptocurrency network ever made. Some of its features, such as the Cardano blockchain and Daedalus wallet, were purpose-built from scratch and designed to be better than anything else currently available.

Primarily based in Japan, it began development in 2015, and was publicly launched on September 29, 2017. Cardano Ada (ADA) tokens were first made available for trading on October 1, 2017. Since then, it's become one of the largest cryptocurrency by market cap, peaking at over US$1.3 billion on November 27, 2017.

One of the main features of the Cardano system is its multi-layer design. There are two key layers to consider:

- **The settlement layer:** This is the layer that operates the ADA tokens.

- **The computing layer:** This layer can run smart contracts, recognize individual users and perform other functions.

Bitcoin and most other cryptocurrencies have all of these functions in one layer. This multi-layer system brings some features that traders may find useful.

- **Upgradeability:** The system has been specifically designed to allow for relatively smooth and easy upgrades with soft forks. The multi-layer design allows for each layer to be forked and upgraded separately.

- **Adaptability:** The computing layer can be adapted in various ways without affecting ADA. For example, it can help to meet different regulatory requirements in different countries without needing to make one-size-fits-all changes to the entire ADA cryptocurrency.

- **Privacy with compliance:** Users can get privacy for their transactions even though the computing layer is able to recognize individuals. This system is designed to offer a level of anonymity while still being compliant with laws.

These layers will be underpinned by the Cardano treasury, which will receive an as yet undecided portion of newly minted Ada and transaction fees.

How is Cardano mined?

Cardano uses an entirely new mining algorithm called Ouroboros. According to its developer, it's the first proof-of-stake mining algorithm that's been mathematically proven to be secure. Most cryptocurrencies use proof-of-work mining, in which miners compete to solve problems, produce the next block and win a reward for doing so. By contrast, proof-of-stake mining works by picking a semi-random stakeholder to solve the next block, with larger stakeholders (contributors with more ADA) more likely to be chosen.

This can potentially offer quicker and cheaper transactions, plus the benefits of being more energy-efficient. The problem is finding a truly reliable and random way to pick the stakeholder to make a block. According to its developers, Ouroboros solves this problem.

Is Cardano trustworthy?

Cardano is entirely open source and patent free. All its source code is publicly available for scrutiny. People interested in Cardano may find that this not only assists development, but also means any problems can be highlighted quickly. It's also fronted and developed by some publicly accessible and widely known names.

- **The Cardano Foundation:** This is a Swiss-based non-profit designed to serve as a standards body for the Cardano protocol as it evolves over time and to interface with regulators in different markets.

- **IOHK:** This is a well-known engineering company dedicated to innovations in peer-to-peer financial services. IOHK is behind most of Cardano's technology.

- **Emurgo:** This is a registered company formed to interface between Cardano and businesses by offering Cardano as a blockchain business solution.

Things to consider before purchasing Cardano

The developers claim that Cardano was purpose-built to be the only cryptocurrency the world needs, offering an exceptional range of features and usefulness. In particular, it's designed to work well with regulations and to be accessible to almost anyone. It has an easy-to-use, dedicated multi-currency wallet and has already laid out plans to release ADA vending machines in Japan.

However, development is still ongoing and its full functions are not going to be available for some time.

Why Cardano could keep growing

Cardano's ADA token managed to leap its market cap from zero to US$18.7 billion across Q4 2017, becoming the fifth most valuable cryptocurrency based on market value. While its growth plateaued like most altcoins following the January 2018 boom, it still may be in a position to be one of the most flexible and viable altcoins moving forward. Here are some reasons why it might continue to grow:

1. **It's one of the most advanced cryptocurrencies:** If you think of bitcoin as a first-generation crypto and Ethereum as a second generation, then Cardano is a third-generation cryptocurrency. It wants to solve the three biggest issues with current coins, which are sustainability, scalability and interoperability. The biggest advantage Cardano holds is its two layers which were mentioned at the start of this chapter. The first layer is the Cardano Settlement Layer (CSL), which works as a much more efficient bitcoin, handling the balance ledger and basic transaction side of things.

   The second layer is the Cardano Computation Layer (CPL). This is where decentralized apps and smart contracts built on Cardano will be based, and it can operate separately to the CSL layer.

   These multiple layers also mean that changes can be made to the platform without a fork. Cardano itself was developed through peer-reviewed academic research and is based on the Haskell programming language, which is viewed as extremely secure and uses mathematical proof of correctness to verify code.

2. **It has a clear, transparent roadmap:** The non-profit Cardano Foundation oversees the majority of community and product development for Cardano, and it regularly updates Cardano's progress. On the Cardano roadmap website, you can see its next major update, Shelley, due in Q2 2018. Shelley is designed to turn Cardano into a fully decentralized and autonomous system.

   After Shelley, they will release the Goguen update, which will introduce a virtual machine and universal language framework. This update will allow third parties to create tokens and more powerful decentralized apps on the platform.

3. **It may become the new Ethereum:** Cardano has the potential to be the new default for decentralized app development and smart contracts, thanks to its ability to scale and handle transactions in a faster way. The platform will also support smart contracts written in Ethereum's Solidity language.

   However, it still faces tough competition from Ethereum. Ethereum is more established and better known, gaining more market share and awareness with every day. The team behind Ethereum is also looking at introducing the Plasma update next year, which will add a second layer solution, allowing Ethereum to handle much larger data sets and help solve some scalability issues. Ethereum's founder believes that this technology will eventually be able to handle the same number of transactions per second as Visa.

   It's important that Cardano is able to establish itself and its final tech before Ethereum gets to this point.

4. **ADA will be available on a network of ATMs in Japan next year:** Japan is currently the largest market in the world for cryptocurrencies, almost triple that of the USA who is in second, with both consumers and businesses showing interest in multiple platforms. The introduction of 25 ATMs will make it much easier for consumers in such a big market to become involved with ADA, raisings its value and bringing it into the mainstream.

5. **The continued crypto hype:** The buzz around cryptocurrencies is expected to keep growing in 2018 as more use cases for blockchain-based technology continue to pop up. The buzz over bitcoin's continued dominance (or not) will attract headlines its value fluctuates in the face of so much new competition. As a result, attention will be brought to other coins for buyers to trade in, particularly those ones that have a sharp rise in value like Cardano enjoyed.

Could Cardano be the next bitcoin?

Cardano's first hurdle is to reach the US$1 mark by the end of 2018. Its continued growth from there depends on whether the development team can hit its targets from the roadmap or even exceed them. When Cardano's feature set expands towards the end of 2018 and it becomes a more powerful platform for smart contracts, it could possibly result in another spike in price.

However, this all depends on Ethereum's growth, too. If Ethereum can implement the likes of Plasma and scale faster before Cardano's platform is ready, it may be too late. It will be worth keeping track of the progress of both cryptos since they will directly influence the value of each other.

Cardano will likely never reach the same price for an individual ADA token as a single BTC due to the 26 billion ADA tokens currently in circulation compared to the 21 million for BTC. However, if the rate of growth continues for Cardano, its total market cap may surpass bitcoin's market cap within the next couple of years.

Cardano's futures launch on BitMEX

As of the start of 2018, traders can purchase futures contracts in ADA, the native token of the Cardano network. The contracts let traders speculate on the future price of the ADA/BTC (Bitcoin) exchange rate. Traders can go long or short on the ADA/BTC exchange rate, meaning that they can bet in favor of the rate increasing or decreasing, depending on their view of the market. At the end of the contract's lifecycle, the trader will receive a payout or debt, according to the success of the contract.

The advantage of such contracts over traditional trading is that the owner of the contract does not need to purchase any of the underlying asset, such as ADA, which increases their exposure to risk. In this instance, the contract is purchased and paid out in BTC, so the trader only needs to purchase BTC in order to take a future position on another coin.

BitMEX also offers traders the option to leverage up to 20 times their initial purchase. So they can effectively borrow up to 20 times the value of their initial BTC purchase. This is called leverage, or margin trading, and is extremely high risk – not for amateurs.

Futures trading has been referred to as the "next wave" of cryptocurrency exchange as it takes a purely speculative stance on the trading of cryptocurrency, whereas traditionally traders might purchase coins because of their intention to use the currency for its intended purpose (transactions, network fees, etc.).

Late in 2017, US financial firms Chicago Board Options Exchange (CBOE) and Chicago Mercantile Exchange (CME) Group began offering bitcoin futures contracts on December 10 and December 18 respectively. They were the first firms to do so, exposing cryptocurrencies to these markets for the first time. These contracts are cash settled, which means the traders never purchase any cryptocurrency themselves.

Futures contracts have been criticized by some veteran cryptocurrency traders as a negative addition to the space since it potentially gives traders a financial incentive to see a coin's price decrease (if they took up a short position). Previously, all traders had benefited from the prices of coins increasing, with the popular adage "a rising tide lifts all boats" often being used to describe market sentiment.

In the days following the release of futures trading, Cardano's price dipped 33%. If you're thinking of buying Cardano, you can see a comparison of exchanges that trade in the token on the finder website.

J – EOS

Symbol: *EIS*
Initial release date: *January 31, 2018*
Encryption algorithm: *Delegated proof of stake (DPoS)*
Max. supply: *1 billion*
Est. total market cap ownership: *1.7%*

EOS is a blockchain platform for the creation of decentralized applications (dapps). With an aim to offer faster transactions and to scale better than Ethereum, it has attracted plenty of interest from across the crypto community. The native token of the EOS platform is (perhaps unsurprisingly) the EOS token (EOS). It is entrenched as one of the world's top 10 cryptocurrencies by market cap as of March 2018, EOS tokens are being distributed through a unique year-long token sale.

EOS isn't an acronym. It's simply what the system is called. Some of the suggestions about what it could stand for are "EOS Operating System" or perhaps less likely "Ethereum on Steroids." Yet, it's the second interpretation that could be attracting many traders. The Ethereum smart contract system has already proven itself, but it isn't very user-friendly and has some scaling problems. Some people believe that by overcoming these, EOS will become the new Ethereum.

EOS is designed to be a much more scalable and easier-to-use version of the extremely popular Ethereum, but with a similar range of functionality. It aims to offer a blockchain network where anyone can participate safely and without any particular technical knowledge. However, it's also focusined on offering a full range of advanced features where desired by its users.

Its specific features include the following:

- A user-friendly software interface for the platform.

- Horizontal and vertical scalability.

- Human-friendly features such as the ability to set delayed transactions.

How does EOS work?

The main feature of EOS is its software. It's designed to make full use of a machine's processing power, such as letting users schedule applications across multiple CPU cores or clusters. This essentially puts a lot more processing power into the blockchain at a much lower cost, while retaining features that are similar to Ethereum, such as smart contracts.

In addition, EOS uses a unique processing algorithm, called delegated proof of stake (DPoS) This is intended to be a more efficient and flexible way of doing things. With these features, you get an advanced blockchain network with advanced functionality, plus no transaction fees and exceptional scalability as well as a system capable to handle millions of transactions per second.

How DPoS works

When blocks are created on a blockchain, they process the transactions. However, someone has to create these blocks at the cost of electricity and processing power. The EOS DPoS system is designed to automate the work, while minimizing the costs involved. It aims to lower them to the extent that the entire network can be run without transaction fees. It does this by ensuring that users are automatically compensated with small amounts of EOS for producing blocks.

There is no set limit on the number of EOS tokens, so the system can theoretically run indefinitely, and the tokens awarded to block creators don't actually have to come from anywhere. They can simply be generated as needed, in a process that imitates very gradual inflation. To prevent tokens from becoming worthless, despite having an unlimited supply, inflation is set at a gradual and predictable amount.

Under DPoS, the system automatically picks block creators from among all users who opt into it. The selection is random, but weighted by the number of EOS tokens a user holds. The more EOS coins someone has, the more likely their collection is to "earn interest" over time as they contribute to the system. This is how the public EOS system works. EOS can also be operated in closed blockchains under admin control. For example, a company might purchase EOS tokens and then distribute them to its administrators to conduct their own transactions on its own network.

What gives EOS tokens value?

The DPoS system means EOS token holders can gradually increase the amount held in their account to help cover the electronic, computing and fees of using the system. Plus, an EOS token buy-in is required to use the system. When the number of users increases quicker than the gradual inflation built into the system, the value of each token may also increase.

What makes EOS so user-friendly?

EOS aims to create a platform that people of any level of experience can use. It does this with a few features in particular.

- **Human-readable account addresses:** EOS permits accounts from 2-32 characters in length that can serve as secure and reliable identifiers.

- **Clearer information:** You won't need programming or other technical knowledge to understand contracts on the blockchain.

- **Reversals and delays:** Contracts can be implemented with a delay, as desired. For example, you might have instant transactions to buy a cup of coffee with EOS, or a week-long cooling-down period when purchasing a house or car.

- **Account restoration:** If a user's account keys are stolen, they can be recovered within 30 days. This is done with a designated account partner who allows the original user to recover their account with two-factor authentication. The idea is that thieves have nothing to gain from recovering an account because they'll only risk exposing themselves for no gain.

- **Separate ecosystems for users:** Businesses might have their own EOS environments customized in their own ways, while the general public might interact in the primary EOS ecosystem.

Things to consider before buying EOS?

Few other cryptos have developed a scalable and sustainable model for rewarding user engagement and operation of the network, and tied it into a user-friendly experience. Ethereum in particular is known to be a useful currency, but hampered by scaling problems and a poor user experience, making it a good foundation for EOS to build on. If it manages to solve these problems successfully, it might become one of the world's main blockchains.

However, it's still in the relatively early stages of development, and some of the main challenges, like a migration to its own blockchain, are still ahead of it. It's also possible that some of the user-friendly features might have unforeseen results and end up being a poor match for user needs on the blockchain.

EOS price prediction

Cryptocurrencies are complicated, speculative and highly volatile. There are many factors that can affect their price, so it's essential to carry out a balanced assessment of those factors to develop a clearer idea of where the price of EOS could be headed in the future. Some of the issues you'll need to take into account are outlined below.

So what could drive EOS's growth?

- **Token sale:** The EOS token sale began on June 26, 2017, and ran for a full year. During the first five days, 200 million tokens were distributed, with 700 million more split evenly into 350 consecutive 23-hour periods of 2,000,000 EOS tokens each. The remaining 10% are set aside for block.one, the company building the EOS.IO software, and cannot be traded or transferred on the Ethereum network.

- **Funding:** While the token sale is taking place, EOS tokens are listed on a number of major cryptocurrency exchanges. Not only does this give people a chance to monitor the development of the project before deciding whether they want to buy in, therefore hopefully increasing adoption, it also allows the project to build a sizable war chest to fund future development.

- **Dan Larimer:** EOS founder Dan Larimer has previously co-founded successful crypto projects Steemit and BitShares and has extensive experience in the cryptocurrency industry.

- **Platform potential:** The EOS platform aims to offer a wide range of features and advantages, including vertical and horizontal scaling of decentralized apps and eliminating user fees. The full list of potential benefits of the platform is too long to list here, so check out the whitepaper for details of what EOS aims to achieve.

- **Active community:** EOS is backed by a very active community and social media following. Check out its Telegram group or its Facebook, Twitter and Steemit pages for evidence, or look at the list of regular EOS meetups around the globe.

- **Ratings:** In its first cryptocurrency rankings released in January 2018, Weiss Ratings gave EOS a B. The only other coin to get the same rating was Ethereum, and none of the 74 coins reviewed scored an A.

- **EOSfinex:** EOS has partnered with Bitfinex to build a decentralized exchange known as EOSfinex. The aim of the project is to provide a fast, transparent and trustless platform for digital asset trading, but there was no official launch date as of July 2018, when it was said to be nearing the end of its initial development.

And what could hold EOS back?

- **Lack of adoption:** There are several platforms in various stages of development that aim to offer scalable dapps. The value of the EOS token will be closely linked to the level of adoption the EOS platform can achieve.

- **Competitors:** Though EOS has been heralded as an "Ethereum killer," the Ethereum platform continues to grow and is the world's second-largest cryptocurrency as of March 2018. EOS faces a huge battle to dethrone Ethereum as the number-one platform for dapps and smart contracts, while it will also need to compete with a host of other projects with similar goals.

- **Still in development:** The EOS platform is still being developed, so it's not yet known for certain whether the technology behind it will be able to deliver on its promise and potential.

- **Losing Dan Larimer:** Some critics of EOS have questioned Dan Larimer's commitment to seeing the project through to fruition. Having developed Steemit and BitShares, and then left for other projects, Larimer has developed a reputation (whether deserved or not) for leaving projects before they're fully developed. If he decides to move on from EOS, this could have an impact on consumer confidence in the platform.

- **No function for tokens:** On its official FAQ page, EOS states that its tokens don't have "any rights, uses, purpose, attributes, functionalities or features, express or implied, including, without limitation, any uses, purpose, attributes, functionalities or features on the EOS Platform." Consider any effect this may have on demand for the token.

What's coming up in EOS's roadmap?

EOS's development team is right in line with the roadmap it released in mid-2017. The EOS Dawn 1.0 release took place in September 2017, while December 2017 saw Dawn 2.0 introduce resource tracking and inter-blockchain communication.

The next stage is Dawn 3.0, which EOS aid in a statement will provide the following benefits: "EOS Dawn 3.0 will re-introduce horizontal scaling of single chains and infinite scaling via secure inter-blockchain communication. With these two features there will be no limit to what can be built on blockchain technology, nor for how decentralized the network of blockchains can become."

As of March 2018, the Dawn 3.0 code was still in the early alpha stage and was not scheduled to be available in a public testnet until the end of Q1 2018. According to the official roadmap, winter 2017 and spring 2018 (northern hemisphere) will see the EOS platform undergo heavy testing with the emphasis on finding security issues and bugs.

Once a stable product has been released, summer and autumn 2018 (northern hemisphere) will see development focus on "optimizing the code for parallel execution."

EOS's competition

Another factor to consider before deciding whether to buy EOS tokens is the competition the EOS network will face from other similar projects. As platforms battle for supremacy and market share in the impending blockchain economy, how EOS stacks up against its competitors could have a positive or negative impact on its price. Competitors to keep an eye out for include the following:

- **Ethereum (ETH):** As of March 2018, Ethereum is currently the biggest and best-known platform for dapps and smart contracts. Launched in July 2015, it's now the world's second-largest cryptocurrency by market cap.

- **NEO (NEO):** Commonly dubbed the Ethereum of China, NEO is an open-source blockchain for the development of smart contracts and digital assets. It's also one of the top 10 cryptocurrencies by market cap as of March 2018.

- **Ethereum Classic (ETC):** Despite being called Classic, ETC was formed from a fork in the original Ethereum blockchain. Ethereum Classic is a decentralized blockchain platform that runs smart contracts.

- **Stratis (STRAT):** Designed to help companies integrate blockchain technology into their systems, Stratis allows companies to create their own custom dapps.

- **Lisk (LSK):** Lisk runs on JavaScript and provides a platform where developers can build custom, industry-specific dapps.

- **Waves (WAVES):** A unique platform that allows startups to run ICOs and also enables the development of dapps, Waves was launched in June 2016.

- **Qtum (QTUM):** Qtum is a China-developed platform that aims to combine Ethereum's smart contracts with bitcoin's secure blockchain.

Beyond 2018: What does the future hold for EOS?

While there seems to be plenty of potential for EOS to enjoy a bright future, there's still a level of uncertainty surrounding the project. The 12 months of 2018 will be a crucial phase for the platform as the much-anticipated official release of the EOS platform occurs.

If it can achieve the goal outlined in its whitepaper of creating "a blockchain architecture that scales to millions of transactions per second, eliminates user fees, and allows for quick and easy deployment of decentralized applications," it could well become a major challenger to the world's second biggest cryptocurrency, Ethereum.

However, there are still a lot of "ifs" at this stage of the project. The EOS platform is still being developed, and big challenges like a stable release and migrating to its own blockchain still lay ahead. And while the platform is being built, competitors like Ethereum are continuing to grow and are also working on solutions to their scaling problems.

Finding out whether EOS has the features and functionality to achieve widespread adoption will be fascinating, so it's definitely a project worth monitoring throughout 2018 and beyond. As it stands, however, EOS is still a relatively new project. While it undoubtedly has a grand vision and plenty of potential, not to mention significant financial backing, whether it will become a viable network that plays a crucial role in the blockchain ecosystem of the future remains to be seen.

If you're thinking of buying EOS, you can see a comparison of exchanges that trade in the token on the finder website.

K – NEO

Symbol: *NEO*
Initial release date: *February 2014*
Encryption algorithm: *Delegated Byzantine Fault Tolerance (dBFT)*
Max. supply: *100 million*
Est. total market cap ownership: *1.2%*

NEO is often considered China's response to Ethereum. Its goal is to create a smarter economy by bridging the gap between digital and traditional assets through the development of smart contracts. NEO began life under the name AntShares, founded by Da Hongfei and his company Onchain. However, in June 2017, it rebranded to NEO.

The platform uses two different tokens (like Ethereum). The first is also called NEO, and the second is called GAS. Both tokens have specific uses on the NEO blockchain platform.

- NEO tokens represent the ownership of the NEO blockchain. They are used to create blocks and manage the network, and when you hold NEO in your wallet, you'll be rewarded with GAS tokens.

- GAS tokens give you the right to use the NEO blockchain. Much like Ether to the Ethereum network, GAS is the fuel that powers transactions in the NEO system. So when you look to make a NEO transaction, the miners that confirm that transaction must be paid a fee – just like with other cryptocurrencies. However, these miners are not paid in NEO, but are instead paid with GAS.

The primary aim of NEO is to become a digital, decentralized and distributed platform for non-digital assets through the use of smart contracts. This means that its goal is to become a digital alternative for asset transfers that are currently non-digital. An example would be paying rent using a smart contract that triggers automatically once a month instead of setting up a bank payment. The contracts can be written in a range of familiar programming languages, including Microsoft.net, Java, Kotlin, Go and Python. These contracts are then integrated into the network by the neoVM compiler.

So what does this mean in the real world? Well, Neo aims to provide the following features:

- **Digital assets:** Through the use of smart contracts, traditional assets can be turned into digital ones and securely stored on the blockchain.

- **Digital identity:** Neo will enable the creation of digital identities for both individuals and organizations, and those identities will only be accessible via multifactor authentication.

- **Smart contracts:** Like Ethereum, Neo will allow the creation of smart contracts. However, Ethereum is based on its own proprietary coding language known as Solidity, which developers must first learn in order to build on the Ethereum ecosystem. Neo supports many additional code bases, thus removing this barrier to entry for developers.

- **Dapps:** Neo will also support the creation of decentralized applications, such as decentralized exchanges and legal smart contracts.

NEO uses the Byzantine Fault Tolerance algorithm when looking to get a consensus on any transactions. This is somewhat similar to the system used by Stellar Lumens. This algorithm can facilitate 10,000 transactions per second, with nodes segregated into their own overlapping networks, and then randomly selected at the time a verification is required. It's worth noting that blockchains that use this algorithm cannot be hard forked.

What sets NEO apart?

The NEO platform, with its system of NEO and GAS tokens, is drastically different from what we know of bitcoin and many other cryptocurrencies. The following are three of the unique differences that set it apart:

1. **NEO indivisible units:** The smallest unit of NEO will always be one share, and this cannot be divided in the same way as other coins like bitcoin. The primary reason for this is that, just like shares in a company or service, NEO cannot be divided into fractions. This might become a problem in the future if NEO's value increases, but exchanges already have their own methods of dividing the coin.

   Exchanges are currently trying to figure out a way around the problem of NEO being indivisible. The answer they have might not be great, but it's the best one we have right now: You'll be allowed to trade fractions of NEO as long as you keep them inside your exchange wallet. If you transfer them to your NEO wallet, those fractions will remain on the exchange and won't be moved to your private wallet.

   For example, you are not technically allowed to own 5.32 NEO. You either have 5 NEO or 6. But exchanges will let you exchange BTC for 5.32 NEO without issue. If you keep those 5.32 NEO in your exchange wallet, you should have no problem exchanging them for another cryptocurrency. However, if you transfer the 5.32 NEO you own to your actual NEO wallet, you will end up with only 5 NEO, and the 0.32 NEO will stay on the exchange.

2. **Generating GAS:** The biggest differentiating feature is the two-tiered system of NEO and GAS. Although GAS can be bought and sold on a handful of exchanges, users typically buy NEO tokens, which represent their stake in the future of the platform. The benefit of the two-tier system comes into play the moment you transfer NEO to your NEO-compatible wallet.

   While holding NEO, you start generating GAS automatically as more blocks are generated by the construction of the blockchain. With every new block generated, eight GAS are distributed for all 100 million NEO in existence.

   This is similar to Ethereum, but very different from mining in bitcoin in that the value of GAS is decoupled from the value of NEO. This is in contrast to bitcoin, where the value of a bitcoin mined is the same as the value of a bitcoin purchased. GAS is used to pay for transaction fees on the NEO network.

3. **Smart contracts:** Another important factor that sets Neo apart from bitcoin is the use of smart contracts, which is best explained using a real-world scenario:

   Smart contracts are the digital equivalent of holding money in escrow with a third party, with the intention of releasing the funds at some point in the future. Suppose I have to pay you 0.002 BTC in three months' time. A contract is created and entered into the blockchain so that it triggers in three months' time as long as I've deposited the required 0.002 BTC.

   Once the contract executes, the money is transferred from my wallet to yours and is automatically witnessed and verified by regulators on the blockchain. However, it's worth noting that that as of March 2018, the fee for deploying a smart contract on the NEO network is 500 GAS.

How to generate GAS

In order to start generating GAS, you can simply buy NEO and hold it in a compatible wallet. This is essentially the same as holding a stake or shares and being paid dividends. On a handful of exchanges, you can buy it directly with fiat currency like US dollars. However, you can also buy NEO with bitcoin, Ether, Litecoin (LTC) and other cryptocurrencies.

So which wallets can hold NEO? Unless you're preparing to place a trade, the security concerns associated with exchange-based wallets mean it's not recommended to hold your funds on an exchange for an extended period of time. Instead, it's generally a safer option to store your NEO in a secure wallet. Things to consider when looking for a good NEO wallet include the following:

What to look for in a NEO wallet

When searching for a NEO wallet that suits your needs, look for the following:

- **NEO and GAS compatibility:** No wallet supports every single available cryptocurrency, so make sure any wallet you choose specifically states that it supports NEO and GAS tokens.

- **Generating GAS:** NEO holders can earn a passive income in much the same way that conventional shareholders in a company can earn dividends. By holding your NEO tokens in an official compatible wallet, you can earn GAS tokens with every new block generated.

- **User-friendliness:** Cryptocurrencies are complicated and confusing, and sometimes the wallets used to store digital coins and tokens have an even higher degree of difficulty. To help make it as easy as possible to manage your funds, look for a wallet that features a simple and intuitive interface.

- **Security features:** To protect your funds, look for a wallet that promises a high-level of security. Offline wallets offer the most protection, but if you're using a desktop, mobile or web wallet, look for features like advanced encryption, two-factor authentication and multisig functionality.

- **Private keys:** The most important security feature of all is whether a wallet allows you to control your private keys. Without a private key, you won't be able to access your crypto holdings, so look for a wallet that allows you to maintain possession of any private keys at all times.

- **Development:** Is the wallet backed by a strong development team? Is the team constantly working to make upgrades and improvements to the wallet?

- **Support:** Check whether the wallet provider has a good reputation for providing prompt and helpful customer support. Check out how you can contact the team and whether support is only available during specific times.

For a comparison of NEO wallets based on all of the above criteria and more, please check the finder website.

Things to know about NEO

As a concept, NEO is relatively complex for most users, especially those new to the world of cryptocurrency. This is one factor which might hamper the adoption of the platform, while there are also other considerations:

- **No share fractions:** One common complaint about this cryptocurrency is that NEO coins are indivisible. Coins like bitcoin avoid this problem by having their coins divisible by up to eight decimal places (the so-called "satoshi"). This means that even as bitcoin gains in value, users can still purchase coins that are within their budget (even though 1 BTC might cost $8,000, one might still buy 10 ⌷BTC for $0.08). This is not something you can do with NEO. If one NEO costs $1,000, you will have to shell out a minimum of $1,000 to get it.

- **Slow to synchronize compared with other currencies:** A second major complaint users have about the platform is that the blockchain is extremely slow to synchronize updates. For example, when transferring NEO from an exchange to your wallet. This might be fixed in the future, but as of the start of 2018, it would be nearly impossible to pay for any large-value transactions that are requiring you to wait for confirmation.

- **Supply:** According to CoinMarketCap, as of March 2018 the circulating supply of NEO was 65,000,000 out of a total supply of 100,000,000 NEO. This should drive up prices, as there isn't much supply, or potential supply, ensuring strong demand.

- **Crowdsale:** 50,000,000 NEO tokens were sold during an August 2017 crowdsale, with the other 50,000,000 reserved until October 16, 2017, to be managed by the Neo Council as follows:

  1. 10,000,000 to Neo developers and Council members.

  2. 10,000,000 as incentives for developers in the Neo system.

  3. 15,000,000 put into auxiliary blockchain projects used by Neo.

  4. 15,000,000 set aside for contingenciesSome commentators have pointed out that reserving half the total supply of NEO tokens for Neo developers produces the potential risk of those tokens being dumped on the market and other practices that could affect NEO's value.

- **Use:** NEO tokens represent the right to manage the network. Management rights include voting for bookkeeping, NEO network parameter changes and a number of other tasks.

- **Proof of stake:** Neo operates on a proof-of-stake model that allows users to generate GAS by staking their NEO tokens in a wallet. GAS is required to perform transactions on the Neo system.

- **Developer use:** One critical factor in the future value of NEO tokens will be the widespread adoption of the NEO platform by developers. While there's been plenty of hype around the potential for NEO in the past 12 months or so, whether it achieves mainstream popularity remains to be seen. We're still waiting for that significant bump in uptake.

- **Based in China:** The fact that NEO is based in China offers both benefits and disadvantages for the coin. On the plus side, China's huge population and economy mean there's great potential for growth if Neo becomes the go-to platform for Chinese developers. On the other side of the coin, the Chinese government has launched a number of crackdowns on cryptocurrencies in the past, so regulatory pressure is a concern.

- **Market competition:** Neo is not only competing with the well-established Ethereum platform, but also with platforms such as Cardano, EOS, Lisk and more.

- **Blockchain outage:** In March 2018, the NEO blockchain went offline for a few hours, creating a lot of debate within the community about its long-term stability. You can read more about NEO's response to that here.

NEO price prediction

Cryptocurrencies are notorious for their volatility, with substantial price fluctuations more or less the norm on global crypto markets. However, these digital currencies are also highly complicated, and there are myriad factors that can potentially have a positive or negative effect on their value. If you're thinking of buying NEO, consider the factors that could drive its price up or down.

So what could drive NEO's growth?

- **Supply and demand:** The maximum supply of NEO is limited to 100 million. As of March 2018, 65 million NEO are in circulation. If the NEO platform can demonstrate its effectiveness for dapps and smart contracts, and achieve widespread adoption, this could lead to increased demand for the tokens.

- **Availability:** NEO tokens can be bought and sold on a wide range of cryptocurrency exchanges. This ease of access provides NEO with increased credibility in the eyes of the general public and also makes it an option for a greater number of people looking to get started in cryptocurrency.

- **Market size:** With a population of more than 1.4 billion people and the second-largest economy in the world, China offers plenty of opportunities for cryptocurrency projects. If NEO can become the platform of choice for Chinese developers, there's definite potential for the NEO token to increase in value.

- **Earning GAS:** Holding NEO in your wallet allows you to earn the NEO network's other native token, GAS, which is used to fuel transactions in the NEO ecosystem. Much like the way some shareholders seek out stocks that pay regular dividends, this ability to earn a passive income from holding NEO may make this currency appealing for some cryptocurrency buyers.

- **ICO success:** In early 2018, the NEO platform was expected to host at least 29 ICOs throughout the following 12 months. If an increasing number of projects choose to run their ICOs through NEO, and if some of those projects can go on to become successful ventures, this could increase demand for the platform.

And what could hold NEO back?

- **Insufficient adoption:** NEO aims to become China's first public blockchain-based cryptocurrency. However, if the platform fails to attract sufficient interest and use from developers - starting in its home country - this could mean bad news for the value of the NEO token.

- **Market competitors:** There are a host of other projects focused on developing platforms for smart contracts and dapps, and NEO will face stiff competition from platforms like Ethereum, EOS and many more. How it stacks up against its competitors will have a big impact on whether it can achieve widespread adoption.

- **Government crackdowns:** In recent times, the Chinese government has been regularly reported to be cracking down on bitcoin, all cryptocurrencies and crypto exchanges. If you're thinking of buying into any China-based crypto project, you'll need to be well aware of the threat posed by regulatory changes.

- **Technological issues:** In March 2018, NEO's blockchain was disrupted by technical issues for a small number of hours. The entire NEO network went down because of issues with a single computer, and this raised questions about the stability of NEO's overall design. It also adds weight to concerns raised by other critics about the platform's centralization.

- **Inability to scale:** Like many other blockchains, one of the key challenges facing NEO in the future will be whether it can effectively scale to handle an increased volume of transactions. NEO's proposed solution to scaling problems, the Trinity Network, is set to be rolled out in 2018.

- **Indivisible:** The smallest unit of NEO is one. While you can buy a fraction of a NEO token on an exchange, you can only move whole NEO tokens between wallets. This is not always desirable.

What's next for NEO?

As interesting a concept as NEO is, there's only one certainty in the future of NEO: no one knows exactly where it's going. Many speculate its value will be high in 2018, but others are not so certain. After all, while the sudden growth in NEO to above US$40 in August 2017 was impressive, it's still very much a mirror of the explosive growth of bitcoin and NEO tumbled back down to around US$23 by September 2017. It turned around in early 2018 and peaked to a new high of over US$80 at the start of the year.

One advantage of NEO is that the Chinese government has embraced the platform, while simultaneously distancing itself from other cryptocurrencies like Ether and bitcoin. This has the potential to both legitimize the NEO platform and alienate it from the Western world. The future of NEO is still very much in flux, and a lot remains to be seen.

The key development in NEO's roadmap for 2018 is the Trinity Network. In much the same way as the Lightning Network aims to improve bitcoin's scalability, Trinity is designed to improve NEO's transaction processing times. Though NEO claims to handle up to 1,000 transactions per second, some critics have suggested that network slowdowns during key ICOs may show this to be untrue.

Trinity will employ state channel technology to enable transactions to be made off-chain, using a multisignature agreement or smart contract. This is designed to allow multiple transactions at the same time, thus increasing transaction speeds and reducing fees. According to the official Trinity roadmap, the network is scheduled for testing on the NEO mainnet in April 2018.

In March 2018, NEO's parent company, Onchain, looked to make stakeholders in the NEO platform more connected with the service. To do that, it distributed one ontology (ONT) token for every five NEO that users of the network held in their wallet. This token isn't one of financial value, but instead allows holders to vote on system upgrades, identity verification and other governance issues surrounding the NEO platform.

Beyond 2018: What does the future hold for NEO?

Looking ahead, 2018 and 2019 will be a fascinating period for NEO and the cryptocurrency industry as a whole. NEO has been the subject of much hype throughout the few years of its existence, and the next couple of years will be crucial as the world waits to see whether the platform can deliver.

The key challenge for NEO will be widespread adoption. There's clearly a huge potential market to tap into, but whether NEO can become the number-one platform for developers in China and further afield remains to be seen. The launch of the Trinity Network will be an important milestone that, if successful, should help future-proof the NEO ecosystem.

However, technical difficulties and outages could impact consumer confidence in the platform, while concerns over centralization will need to be addressed. NEO will also face significant competition from a host of other smart contract platforms, too – most notably Ethereum. Of course, each of its competitors faces its own challenges and opportunities.

The other key factor to monitor closely is the threat of government regulation. China is notoriously strict on cryptocurrencies, so regulatory changes and crackdowns are always a concern. However, NEO has been built to comply with all local regulations, so it may be well placed to ride out any political turmoil.

To get started, review the exchanges on the finder website and decide which one you would like to use.

L – IOTA

Symbol: *MIOTA*
Initial release date: *June 21, 2014*
Encryption algorithm: *Curl*
Max. supply: *2,779,530,283*
Est. total market cap ownership: *1.1%*

The driving force behind IOTA is the rapidly growing network of interconnected devices termed the Internet of Things or IoT. IOTA's goal is to provide an infrastructure that enables machine-to-machine transactions to happen between all the different devices that are hooked into the Internet. At the core of this goal is an innovative new spin on the blockchain, called the Tangle.

The Tangle builds on the idea of a distributed ledger, a central component of today's blockchains, and has emerged as a new kind of data structure. It's a decentralized, peer-to-peer network that does not rely on blocks, mining or an external consensus process. This allows secure data transfers to happen directly between digital devices, without transaction fees, in a self-regulating manner. It also means it is infinitely scalable.

IOTA's Tangle architecture is designed to manage transactions in the rapidly growing digital economy that undergirds the so-called Internet of Things (IoT). The vast majority of the devices that are connected to the Internet, such as computers, are not running at their full capacity most of the time. Many people use computers for things like checking email or browsing the web, but behind the scenes their computers could be doing a lot more without impacting performance.

Part of IOTA's vision is to provide a secure way for people to earn money by letting others access some of that unused power. In the real world, the potential for this new machine-to-machine economy spans far beyond personal computers. IOTA plans to be the backbone of a new kind of sharing economy designed for a wide variety of smart devices, including mobiles.

The IOTA cryptocurrency is one aspect of the larger IOTA platform. Designed with mass adoption in mind, IOTA hopes to provide a foundation for digital transactions to occur throughout the Internet of Things. The IOTA cryptocurrency is intended to serve as a universal method of payment for the future of machine-to-machine transactions that happen on the IOTA network.

This is quite different from the bitcoin cryptocurrency. Bitcoin introduced two fundamental concepts to the world: decentralized digital currencies and the blockchain. IOTA has built upon both of those ideas to create a new kind of infrastructure designed for the expanding network of Internet-connected machines or smart devices. Instead of focusing on peer-to-peer transactions, like bitcoin, IOTA is designed primarily for transactions that happen on a machine-to-machine level.

There are a lot of possibilities when it comes to how IOTA will be used. Smart cars, energy grids, tools, drones and personal computers are all examples of things that potentially integrate into the IOTA architecture. Creating an open market for resources to be shared among devices connected to the Internet of Things may be the primary goal of IOTA, but there are other potential uses also being explored. Because secure data transfer is central to IOTA, research is being done into the potential for electronic voting and governance to make use of this technology.

The public organization behind IOTA is called the IOTA Foundation. The most important members of the foundation are David Sønstebø, Dominik Schiener, Serguei Popov and Sergey Ivancheglo. You can learn more about what IOTA is about by watching finder's interview with the IOTA Foundation's Giorgio Mandolfo on the finder website.

Blockchain vs Tangle

So what is the difference between the blockchain technology that most cryptocurrencies use and the Tangle system employed by IOTA? Both are what they sound like. A blockchain is like a chain of blocks, while the Tangle is more like a web.

There is a problem with blockchains. Transactions on a blockchain are built in a chain and transacted as they come. In most cases, these transactions are processed by miners who lend their computing power to the blockchain and get rewarded with the blockchain's cryptocurrency for doing so. This reward is partly from newly released coins, but mostly from transaction fees.

The blocks with the highest transaction fees get processed first because they're the most valuable to miners. And if there are more transactions waiting than can currently be processed, they're put in a backlog. As such, when a blockchain gets busier and more popular, transactions on it get slower and more expensive. This can be seen to varying degrees in many popular blockchain-based cryptocurrencies.

This is known as the scaling problem because it might put a hard limit on how big and valuable a cryptocurrency can get before it becomes so slow and expensive that it's not worth using. Many people believe that the only way a cryptocurrency can truly become a useful global currency is by solving the scaling problem. So how does Tangle solve it?

Tangle doesn't use miners, and it doesn't use a blockchain. Instead, it uses a "directed acyclic graph" system. This is basically a fancy way of calling it a web. Each device on the Tangle (such as a PC, a phone or anything else connected to the network) will be able to make and process its own transactions. To make a transaction, a device needs to process two other transactions on the Tangle.

It does this with easy proof-of-work algorithms. The idea is that almost any device with a computer chip has a lot of processing power, and that it's mostly going to waste. By putting that power to work and having every transaction verify and process two other transactions, Tangle aims to solve the scaling problem.

What is the IOTA Ecosystem?

One of the more recent developments with IOTA is the announcement and subsequent funding of the IOTA Ecosystem initiative. The IOTA Ecosystem isn't just a place to develop IOTA applications; it's a major application in its own right. The Ecosystem has been announced, but not yet released.

"The IOTA Ecosystem will be ground-zero for permissionless, distributed and decentralized technology striving to build a more inclusive, resilient and prosperous world," announced the IOTA Foundation. To grow and sustain the system in the future, users have donated about $37 million worth of IOTA. This will be used to reward developers, creators and other contributors in the Ecosystem.

Although the IOTA Foundation is still running the show, the IOTA Ecosystem has been set up to be as sustainably transparent and decentralized as possible.

"While the IOTA Foundation will lead the IOTA Ecosystem, we aim to have its development, management and governance be a community driven effort. Through broadcasted proposals and direct voting on the Tangle, the broader community will be able to nominate new initiatives, vote on important decisions, and help guide the Ecosystem's maturation. As the Ecosystem grows and expands, we will be calling on community members to manage various focus areas of the Ecosystem as well as propose and develop new ones."

Like many decentralized communities, IOTA has decided to create a self-managing democratic digital utopia. Unlike most, it can use the Tangle system to have a better chance of succeeding. The IOTA Ecosystem is being designed to allow for transparent management of funds, and an almost completely community-directed experience. To this end, it will incorporate the following Tangle-based features:

- A voting system.

- A program to nominate new proposals and initiatives.

- Contributor competitions.

- Community-directed funding and rewards systems.

- Transparent benchmarks, performance criteria and accountability metrics for Ecosystem contributors.

- A reputation system.

"A decentralized reputation system will be implemented. Through this anyone in the IOTA community can share their voice in favor or against the trustworthiness of IOTA Ecosystem contributors and the quality of their work via transactions on the Tangle. This will make accountability in the Ecosystem fully transparent and devoid of any kind of capricious third-party intervention."

It may be safe to assume that the reputation system will be abused by many community members to the fullest extent possible as a tool to undermine the confidence of one's rivals and to stamp out competing projects wherever possible, especially when there's money or ideology at stake. On the plus side, this inevitable systemic abuse will be completely transparent and hard to keep getting away with.

The Ecosystem Development Fund (EDF) consists of roughly US$38 million. This money was previously donated by community members with the eventual goal of supporting the Ecosystem. These funds will be distributed by the community to the community.

"To ensure the IOTA community has their voices heard with respect to how EDF funds are spent, we are working on building a program where community members can nominate and vote for new proposals and initiatives. This occurs through a procedure that takes place entirely on the Tangle."

Projects will be assessed on the Tangle in line with tangible performance criteria. "By memorializing EDF funding agreements with 'Proof-of-Existence' transactions on the Tangle, anyone will be able to verify that agreements the EDF enters existed in a certain state at a certain point in time. The IOTA community can thus hold both the EDF and the benefactors of EDF funds accountable to their commitments," the foundation explains.

"To be able to learn from our successes and failures, all Ecosystem initiatives and financial support awarded by the EDF will have a series of metrics and indicators that can be used to monitor and evaluate the Ecosystem and EDF's effectiveness and performance over time. These could include both qualitative and quantitative measures to evaluate project results, initiatives, and the like. This data will be broadcast on the Tangle so that everyone can evaluate the effectiveness of the program and make recommendations and vote for changes to improve the IOTA Ecosystem and the EDF for years to come."

As of Mid 2018, the IOTA Ecosystem is not yet able to begin funding projects, but the features you should be able to find after launch include the following:

- Resources in the form of tutorials, videos and other interactive learning materials for users and creators.

- Developer resources like new libraries, modules and second-layer applications.

- Matchmaking organizations, partnered startups and other people with the kind of expertise and reputation you're looking for.

- News, articles and other posts related to the development of pilots, new applications and other updates.

- Hackathons and other IOTA Ecosystem-sponsored competitions and events.

- Philanthropic initiatives for positive social and environmental impact.

- Updates on current Ecosystem work and EDF status, for transparency.

- A landing page, which appears to be the only fully functional feature in the Ecosystem as of March 2018.

The IOTA Ecosystem has a number of intriguing implications that might significantly expand the potential applications of IOTA beyond its current scope.

Wider application of Tangle benefits: The measurable and transparent performance criteria of all EDF-funded projects could be applied to other philanthropic initiatives. The IOTA Ecosystem could be a ready-to-go gold standard for charitable organizations and a place for groups to take their work and fundraising plans.

An exceptionally efficient workflow paradigm: The IOTA Ecosystem's built-in transparency, incentive system and decentralized community-driven management structure has the potential to be a new workflow paradigm, which is able to minimize duplication of effort, assign tasks to the best team for the job and use a type of crowd wisdom to effectively prioritize tasks and determine strategy.

Organic machine learning: The IOTA Ecosystem is looking a lot like a crowd-sourced machine-learning system. It's built to evolve, learn from its successes and mistakes as a community, keep building on previous developments and generally become more effective over time. Depending on how well it works, the IOTA Ecosystem might be one of the first systems to effectively and organically apply crowd wisdom to its ongoing development. Combined with the above benefits, this might translate into the exceptionally quick development of an exceptionally varied and high quality range of IOTA applications.

IOTA in action with Kontrol Energy

A new IOTA-affiliated branch is opening in Toronto, Canada through a partnership with Kontrol Energy Corp. It's called the bIOTAsphere, and the new offices will serve as the IOTA Foundation's primary Canadian office.

This arm of IOTA is expected to focus primarily on reducing the energy costs, reducing emissions and generally providing more sustainable and cost-effective energy solutions for partners and participants through distributed ledger technology (DLT) and other advances.

"We intend to participate in the bIOTAsphere project as an official partner while engaging some of our partner companies in this co-innovation exercise," said IOTA's Dominik Schiener. It's safe to assume that many of IOTA's partners are eager to explore the possibilities of distributed ledger technology in energy and might be able to benefit from a connection to the bIOTAsphere.

The stated goals of the bIOTAsphere include the following:

- Facilitating "a Net-Zero emission world through the application of IOTA in the energy and carbon markets."

- Facilitating "the commercialization of IOTA applications and to educate stakeholders in North America and globally about the value of the DAG based Tangle to solve some of the world's large and complex problems."

- Minimizing the environmental impact of current technological developments.

The bIOTAsphere will be a non-profit collaborative environment for individuals and institutions to offer and receive assistance. In particular, it aims to facilitate exceptionally rapid development of IOTA solutions, similar to the IOTA Ecosystem. Members are obligated to check in with a bIOTAsphere liaison at least once a month and commit to sharing progress reports with other bIOTAsphere members.

"We're committed to ensuring that we create a collaborative and open workspace that encourages innovation and sharing with the highest levels of integrity," reads the bIOTAsphere explainer.

IOTA in action with Taiwan Citizen ID cards

IOTA has partnered with the city of Taipei to help create a smart city based on the IOTA network's Tangle ledger. One of the first steps is the issuance of Tangle-based ID cards to the citizens of Taipei, the IOTA Foundation reports.

"The first project will be digital citizen cards with built-in TangleID. As Taipei City's Smart City Living Lab opens to proof-of-concept projects, IOTA's ultimate secure distributed ledger technology could help Taipei City's digital citizen cards from being tampered with, allowing citizens to feel at ease without worrying about identity theft or fraud when voting, providing background medical information or using any government-related service."

Distributed ledger-based identification cards provide a wide range of use cases. "It is great to see IOTA's technology implemented in a variety of scenarios that will offer true value," said IOTA Foundation co-founder Dominik Schiener.

The potential applications of a Tangle-based ID card system might be further expanded when connected to other smart city systems. Taipei City has already been trialing the "Airbox" data marketplace system. This takes the form of hundreds of small sensors, currently found in homes around the city and 150 Taipei City elementary schools. These detect temperature, humidity, light and pollution. Together, they're one of the most comprehensive environmental sensor networks on the planet.

The data they're collecting will be put on Tangle to create an incentivization platform for the sharing of this information and to help with live air pollution monitoring. This will be used by all PM2.5 stations (particulate air pollution measurement stations) in Taiwan.

IOTA isn't the only cryptocurrency launching smart city trials in 2018. IoT competitor Waltonchain has partnered with a subsidiary of China's state telecom service to roll out smart city trials in Zhangzhou, and ICON's 2018 roadmap shows a modular shift towards smart cities in Korea.

IOTA price prediction

If you're thinking of buying IOTA, there's plenty of factors to consider. Let's start by looking at what could drive up IOTA's growth?

- **Commercial partnerships:** IOTA has partnered with Volkswagen, Bosch, Samsung and a host of other big names in the corporate world. As mentioned, it has also partnered with the city of Taipei to give its citizens Tangle-based ID cards.

- **Use cases:** From web payments and remittances to smart cities, supply-chain management and public transport, there are many potential real-world uses for IOTA technology.

- **Growth potential:** IOTA is designed as a platform for the Internet of Things (IoT), which is predicted to be worth $267 billion by 2020 and have 20.4 billion connected "things" by this same date. If IOTA can provide a successful alternative to the blockchain for IoT, there's a sizable market that could be tapped into.

- **Scalability:** Unlike many blockchains that are encountering issues with their slower transaction times and relatively higher fees, the IOTA network is designed to be infinitely scalable.

- **Supply:** The maximum supply of 2,779,530,283 MIOTA is already circulating within the community. Also remember that one IOTA is the currency's smallest divisible portion, and one MIOTA equals one million IOTA. Make sure you consider the effects this could have on the supply/demand equation for this cryptocurrency in the near and far future.

- **IOTA Ecosystem:** The IOTA Ecosystem is a platform for developers, startups, hobbyists and initiatives around the world working on applications built on the IOTA core protocol. According to the concept's creators, the Ecosystem will be "a hub of education, innovation, tools, collaboration and development for the IOTA distributed ledger protocol."

And what could hold IOTA back?

- **Still in development:** The technology behind the IOTA platform is still in the early stages of development. Whether the Tangle is ready for mainstream implementation and will be able to achieve a sufficient level of widespread adoption remains to be seen.

- **New tech:** The Tangle architecture, which is central to IOTA, is a new kind of data structure. As with any new technology, there is no way to know how it will work in the real world until it's implemented.

- **Competition:** The ability of any new technology to achieve successful adoption will in part depend on how it stacks up against its competitors. For example, IOTA will need to compete with platforms like Ethereum and IoT Chain for market share moving forward.

- **Availability:** As of March 2018, MIOTA was only listed on a handful of cryptocurrency exchanges. Being successfully listed on a wider range of exchanges could potentially increase the currency's visibility and credibility, therefore driving demand.

- **Public perception of alleged security flaws:** In September 2017, the MIT-affiliated Digital Currency Initiative reported that it had uncovered a vulnerability in IOTA's code. This claim was later debunked in a bombshell email leak, and as of March 2018, it appeared that IOTA was actually completely secure. However, the effect of the scandal could have a long-term impact on widespread perception of the security of the platform.

What's ahead on IOTA's roadmap?

One key way to determine what developments a company has in store for the future, and what impact those developments might have on a currency's value, is to take a look at its roadmap. Unfortunately, as of March 2018, IOTA's next roadmap was still being prepared. However, some key goals for 2018 can be found in this 2018 preview published on the official IOTA blog.

Growth of the IOTA Foundation: Established in 2017, the foundation aims to ensure sufficient human resources and capacity to meet the demand for IOTA. According to the blog post, "establishing proper structure and streamlined processes, as well as onboarding tens of new developers and other vital human resources, will be the number one priority at the beginning of 2018."

- **Optimization:** 2018 will see the implementation of a range of developments designed to optimize IOTA, with the goal of "reaching a production ready state by the end of 2018 and begin the international standardization process together with the industry." IOTA will also host several virtual and physical hackathons throughout the year to encourage further development around the IOTA protocol.

- **New offices:** IOTA has plans for seven new offices in locations around the world.

- **Integration with new exchanges.** Here is a statement from an IOTA blog post; "We are now happy to confirm that several large and small exchanges are done with the technical implementation of IOTA. From here on it is up to the respective parties as businesses to decide when and how they plan to unveil and launch IOTA on their various platforms. But we do expect most businesses to do this in the very beginning of 2018."

IOTA has set the ambitious goal of leapfrogging blockchain technology with a significantly better system. Plus, it won't be minting any new coins. As it's more widely adopted, the typically traded amounts might turn from MIOTA to KIOTA to IOTA.

A lot of different stakeholders are also taking an interest. IOTA has announced some high-profile partnerships with various brands, including Microsoft, Samsung, Cisco and Volkswagen, while others are already building new technologies with the specific intention of migrating them to the IOTA network later on.

It's also worth considering that the potential applications of a successful Tangle network are almost infinite. The following are some of the applications floated by various organizations:

- **Leasing anything in real time:** If it can be powered and fitted with a computer chip, it can run on the network.

- **Sharing processing power:** Seamlessly sharing processing power between computers, phones and other devices.

- **Permanently solving car problems:** By giving new cars a digital twin on the Tangle network, vehicles can be tracked in detail in every way. Car theft, odometer tampering, failure to disclose previous accidents and more would potentially be a thing of the past.

- **Locating and reuniting people:** IOTA has already partnered with the non-profit organization Refunite, testing its fee-free distributed ledger system with the organization's missing person database.

- **E-governance:** It could be a secure, low-cost and tamper-proof way for populations to vote and participate in government.

- **Communication:** It presents a more secure and cost-effective way of communicating through phones, computers and anything else.

With almost limitless applications and ambitious technology that is rapidly improving, many people think that IOTA might be the way of the future. However, it's hard to predict the future role of the coin in the Tangle network. It's been described as an instrument to help machines speak with each other rather than something to pass between human hands. Its uniqueness makes it hard to predict what IOTA "should" be valued at and how well it will store value in the long run.

It's also worth considering the possibility of other tokens operating on the IOTA Tangle network in the future. The network itself might be the main attraction. The IOTA token, which isn't necessarily meant for human hands, might end up being one of the least valuable coins available on it.

IOTA's competition

IOTA's price will also be influenced, both positively and negatively, by the actions of its competitors. Before deciding whether you should buy IOTA, consider the challenges the project will face from the following competitors:

- **Ethereum (ETH):** Blockchain platform Ethereum allows developers to build and deploy decentralized applications (dapps) and create smart contracts. Its native token, Ether (ETH), is the world's second-largest cryptocurrency by market cap as of March 2018. While the development teams behind IOTA and Ethereum have clashed on multiple occasions, Ethereum has the key advantage of being an established player with existing infrastructure in place.

- **IoT Chain (ITC):** Created by a Singapore startup, the Internet of Things Chain aims to develop a blockchain-based operating system that provides for the safe communication between devices on the IoT. Its native token, ITC, began trading in December 2017, but the technology behind the project is not scheduled to be fully developed until 2019.

- **Nano (XRB):** Originally starting life as RaiBlocks, Nano combines blockchain and directed acyclic graph (DAG) technology with the aim of providing an instant, fee-free scalable currency. While this project has a different focus than IOTA, the two currencies will compete with each other in specific areas, such as micropayments.

- **Hut43 (Entropy):** Developed in Sydney, Australia, the Hut43 Project looks to connect chatbots and the data produced by IoT devices into one network so that information can be more accessible and even monetized by the data's owners.

Beyond 2018: What does the future hold for IOTA?

Cryptocurrencies are complex and speculative, and predicting their success (or otherwise) is a high-risk guessing game. This is particularly the case with IOTA and its unique Tangle architecture. While Tangle could be a competitor to blockchain and offer benefits in a wide range of use cases, it's not yet certain whether it will be able to deliver on its potential.

As with any new technology, only once it's been rigorously tested and successfully used in several real-world cases can we know for sure whether it provides a useful solution. Experts are predicting the IoT to be a huge growth sector – Google's acquisition of smart home automation company Nest for $US3.2 billion in 2014, not to mention IBM's US$200 million investment in the Watson IoT are evidence of this. However, IOTA is still being developed and consolidating after a year of rapid growth in 2017, so while there is plenty of potential upside, it will also be very interesting to see what the next 12 months hold.

If you're thinking of buying IOTA, the main point to remember is that the technology backing the network is relatively new and still being developed and tested. If it works as planned, the Tangle could become a viable competitor to blockchain technology and could find itself well placed to take advantage of the forecast growth in the IoT sector.

However, IOTA's technological framework has copped criticism from some quarters, so do your own research into how it works before deciding whether you should buy this particular digital currency.

If you're thinking of buying IOTA, you can see a comparison of exchanges that trade in the token on the finder website.

M – MONERO

Symbol: *XMR*
Initial release date: *April 18, 2014*
Encryption algorithm: *CryptoNight*
Max. supply: *Unlimited*
Est. total market cap ownership: *1%*

If you're looking for a secure, anonymous and untraceable currency, you may want to consider Monero. Monero (XMR) appears to have become synonymous with anonymity and secure transactions. While many people believe that bitcoin is already anonymous, this is definitely not the case as we'll see in this guide. The anonymous nature of bitcoin is very much up for debate and Monero is the natural outcome of that debate.

Monero can trace its origins back to 2012 when Bytecoin, the first real-life use of the Cryptonote application layer protocol, was launched. However, the Bytecoin blockchain was later forked and, in April 2014, BitMonero was launched. This release was the result of a need identified by developers to make a more secure, anonymous and untraceable cryptocurrency. BitMonero was later renamed to just Monero. It presents itself as having three core values:

- **Security:** Without trust, no cryptocurrency can survive and none of them are more reliant on that trust than Monero. Its users not only trust it with their money but also with keeping their transactions anonymous.

- **Privacy:** Monero claims it needs to be able to protect its users' anonymity, even in a court of law, including "in extreme cases, from the death penalty."

- **Decentralization:** Monero isn't run by anyone. It's unlike some other coins where there's a central agency that runs the network or blockchain. In the case of Monero, not only does this central, controlling agency or business not exist, but the development decisions and the developer meeting logs are published and available online for anyone to see.

How is Monero's anonymity different from bitcoin?

Monero focuses on anonymity, and this is where it diverges significantly from bitcoin. Many believe that bitcoin is anonymous, but that's a common misconception.

Bitcoin is built over what is known as the public ledger or blockchain. This was done so that users of bitcoin can verify other people's transactions, especially in cases where these payments need to be transparent (e.g., government spending and not-for-profit organizations (NPOs).

The issue is that once you share your bitcoin address, all past and future transactions and how much money you're sending/receiving will always be linked with you. Buyers may not always find this desirable. It's not only an issue of revealing that users may be purchasing or paying for illegal services/products. You just might not want your employer to know that you sent money to WikiLeaks, or maybe you don't want to have freelance clients know how much you're charging other clients.

Bitcoin's solution: Bitcoin came up with a somewhat temporary solution. The idea is that whenever you're requesting money from someone, you should always provide them with a temporary wallet address. This address is related to your actual wallet, but would be a one-time-use address and then would be destroyed, making it harder to trace your wallet's main address back to you. This solves the problem for one-off payments, but organizations and businesses who want a public address visible on their website, for example, would still have all their transactions traceable back to them.

Monero's solution: Monero's solution to this problem is to use what is known as ring signatures, ring confidential transactions and stealth addresses. Monero mixes the address for a user's transactions with other users' addresses, making the path between sender and receiver virtually untraceable. Analysis of the Monero blockchain would reveal nothing more than a cryptographic hash of the transaction. This is termed a ring signature.

In addition, Monero employs Ring Confidential Transactions (RingCT), which obscure the amount sent. Finally, and similar to bitcoin's suggested solution, Monero hides addresses behind one-time-use ones. These so-called stealth addresses are then destroyed so that the transaction cannot be traced back to a public address.

This high level of privacy also means that Monero offers fungibility, which means that every coin has equal value and is interchangeable. Because no two Monero coins are distinguishable from one another, this removes the risk of XMR being refused by vendors or exchanges due to their association in previous transactions, for example theft.

What to watch out for with Monero

No cryptocurrency is without its concerns and Monero is no different.

- **Mining centralization:** Mining is currently controlled by four large pools. While no particular pool controls more than 20% of the entire Monero hash rate, this is still a problem as decentralization is of utmost importance. Luckily, the Monero development team has stated that this is as important to them as to Monero users. Because a hack on a blockchain requires convincing 51% or more of the users that your data is the correct one, with only four large pools you would only need to hack three mining pools to control 60% of the blockchain, at which point you control the entire blockchain.

- **Large transactions:** Because Monero has to add overhead to every transaction to make sure they're anonymous and secure, the system is quite noticeably slower and the transactions are larger and consume more space on a user's computer.

- **Is it anonymous?** In a recent paper, researchers claim to be able to trace around 80% of Monero transactions or to be able to trace transactions with over 80% certainty, depending on how you look at it. This traceability comes due to a potential vulnerability in Monero's privacy algorithm. Monero uses a system of mixins. These are coins that are mixed in as chaff with the actual transaction. The system essentially takes a number of other Monero transactions of the same denomination and lines them up alongside the real transaction. The idea is that this makes it impossible to tell which transaction is the real one. The problem is that researchers say they can look at the line-up and pick out the real transfer among the mixins most of the time.

- **They claim you can look at the age of each transaction:** For about 80% of transactions, the one with the youngest coin age (time since last transaction) is the real one over 90% of the time. So when in doubt, they say one can pick the real transaction with much better-than-even odds simply by picking the "youngest" one. Is this a real vulnerability? And if so, can it be fixed?

Monero's hard fork

Monero has more reasons to fight centralization than most, and is hitting at ASIC mining to do it. Decentralization isn't just a buzzword. It's a very real function in cryptocurrency with tangible impacts. In the case of proof-of-work cryptocurrencies where coins are mined by processing power, an entity with enough hashing (mining) power could gain control of the entire network. In a large enough network, this is extremely unlikely because you'd need an unfeasibly huge amount of hashing power to do it.

But you might also run into problems when the mining power isn't sufficiently diverse. For example, if too much is in one physical location then an earthquake might knock it out or remove enough power for someone else to seize control of the network. Or if most of the hashing power comes from one type of hardware, then that might also be a centralized point of failure. This is what Monero's concerned with, and why it's planning a hard fork on April 30, 2018 into what will be called MoneroV.

A hard fork is essentially a type of blockchain software upgrade. It's called a fork because it essentially diverts the network down a new path. Those who don't follow the new path will be left on the old prong, with a cryptocurrency that's no longer the "official" version. These are usually done fairly painlessly, but sometimes coins will schism if they can't agree which path to follow.

If you are a Monero holder, there's nothing you need to do. You might not even know it's happened. If you're a Monero node operator, you will need to upgrade to the newer software, just as you might have done many times before.

What this fork does

This Monero fork will change Monero's CryptoNight proof-of-work algorithm to prevent it from being effectively mined by application specific integrated circuit (ASIC) hardware. It also introduces the MimbleWimble protocol that allows for greater scalability.

ASIC hardware is purpose-built to be extremely good at certain tasks – in this case, mining cryptocurrencies. If too many people start mining Monero with ASIC hardware, the network risks becoming too centralized. Most normal people cannot afford the ASIC hardware used by the top miners.

The CryptoNight algorithm was designed to encourage mining with CPUs and GPUs, your everyday home computer parts, instead. By limiting the effectiveness of ASIC hardware and encouraging mining with CPUs and GPUs, the network can remain decentralized and more secure as it is achievable by a wider range of people. The combination of anonymity, value and CPU/GPU-mineability is why Monero is usually the chosen cryptocurrency by those involved in crypto jacking.

The bitcoin network has been largely given over to ASIC mining, but Monero might have more reason to be concerned. It's designed for absolute anonymity and has gotten a justified reputation as one of the preferred currencies for illegal purchases, such as for the North Koreans or for anyone else that wants their money to remain untraceable. Authorities have many good reasons to want Monero gone, and ASIC hardware presents one of the most likely avenues for this.

This is because there are very few manufacturers able to produce ASIC hardware in a cost-effective manner. ASIC mining also leads to physical consolidation of hashing power and bitcoin-style cryptocurrency mining farms. A coin like Monero naturally wants to avoid having its network run across a small handful of physical locations where someone could attack the network by kicking a few doors in. That would go against the entire core of operating on blockchain technology.

Monero price prediction

Monero should be watched for its growth potential and whether the developers are placing a focus on decentralization and security.

We are told that a bigger effort to push adoption by merchants, especially in certain areas of the world where adoption has been slow, and a better platform for developers to build upon is in the works.

Monero's privacy features were a key factor in seeing its value rise from around US$10 at the start of 2017 to US$350 by the end of the year. However, in a crowded privacy coin market, does Monero have the features and functionality needed to achieve further growth, or is its price headed for a dip?

So what could drive Monero's growth?

- **Supply:** The initial supply of Monero is approximately 18.4 million coins, after which time there will be a permanently fixed production of 0.3 XMR per minute forever to counteract the number of lost coins per year. As of March 2018, CoinMarketCap reported the circulating supply of XMR at 16 million.

- **Demand:** The sheer number of coins targeting private transactions would seem to indicate that anonymity is a key concern for many cryptocurrency users. The popularity of such currencies also indicates that there is demand for privacy coins, and this is the market which Monero is aiming to tap into.

- **Privacy and anonymity:** While some coins only offer a limited level of anonymity or provide private transactions as an optional feature, Monero's key goal is to offer private and untraceable transactions. This is a unique selling point that sets it apart from many other coins.

- **Increased regulation:** As legislators and law enforcement agencies have battled to keep pace with the rise of cryptocurrency, this has seen an increase in the ability to track transactions using bitcoin and other coins. As a result, users who value their privacy may be forced to search for a coin that offers a higher level of anonymity, such as Monero.

- **Its history:** Monero has been around since 2014 and has established a reputation as a secure and anonymous currency with trusted privacy features. This could help it fight off challenges from other, newer competitors.

- **MoneroV:** On April 30, 2018, a new cryptocurrency known as MoneroV will be created from a Monero hard fork. The new coin integrates the MimbleWimble protocol with the aim of being fully scalable. At the time of the fork, XMR holders will receive MoneroV tokens at a rate of 1:10. This was one factor contributing to a recent XMR price rise during early 2018.

And what could hold Monero back?

- **Competition:** There are plenty of other cryptocurrency projects focused on providing private transactions as standard or as an optional feature. Zcash, Verge and Dash are just a few of the competitors that could potentially challenge Monero for market share.

- **Ties to illegal activity:** Every coin that places an emphasis on private transactions inevitably ends up being linked with criminal activity, which can hamper a coin's widespread public perception and impact upon its level of adoption. For example, Monero has been exploited in cryptocurrency mining operations, while it's also been reported to have become the currency of choice for criminals on the dark web. Even North Korea has been reportedly mining Monero and stealing it by hacking servers in South Korea.

- **Increased regulation:** Another factor to consider is that governments in several countries around the world are regularly reported to be planning "crackdowns" on cryptocurrency. Due to their perceived connection to illegal activity, privacy coins could well be the target of any new legislation. Of course, whether coins like Monero could sidestep any new regulations remains to be seen.

- **Scalability:** Monero's critics have pointed to potential issues with the currency's scalability, as the privacy technologies used increase the size of Monero transactions, which could lead to slower processing times and higher transaction fees in the future. However, Monero's developers are looking at ways to work around this issue such as with the April 2018 fork.

- **Mining centralization:** Critics have also suggested that the centralization of Monero mining exposes it to the risk of someone else seizing control of the network. However, Monero plans to combat this problem with its hard fork.

Beyond 2018: What does the future hold for Monero?

Unlike many other cryptocurrencies, Monero is private by default and has been designed with private and anonymous transactions at the top of its list of goals. This fact alone should stand it in good stead, as history has shown that there's certainly demand for a coin that allows secret transactions.

However, Monero's privacy is something of a double-edged sword. While its untraceable nature makes it an attractive proposition for anyone who wants to transact anonymously, this also makes the coin a suitable choice for anyone who operates outside the law. This could severely hamper the mainstream public perception of Monero, while it also raises the risk of potential regulatory changes.

There are also the aforementioned challenges of scalability, which Monero is actively seeking to solve. Ultimately, Monero is an established coin with a solid reputation for providing secure and anonymous transactions, so it is well positioned for the battle that lies ahead. If the Monero community can successfully tackle scaling issues before they become major problems, and without impacting on XMR's privacy features, this should mean good things for Monero moving forward.

For a full comparison of the exchanges that sell Monero, check the finder website.

N – TRON

Symbol: *XMR*
Initial release date: *September 2017*
Encryption algorithm: *N/A*
Max. supply: *100 billion*
Est. total market cap ownership: *1%*

TRON is a much-talked-about project that aims to use blockchain technology to construct a global free-content entertainment system. Launched in 2017, its native token, Tronix (TRX), has experienced substantial fluctuations, including a growth of 3,650% in the space of just one month.

TRON aims to create a fully decentralized Internet by facilitating a fully functional user-centric ecosystem. It was built in response to the perception of users losing control of the Internet, under arguments that social media giants, advertisers and other large sites have taken control and that content creation is motivated purely by profit, rather than by artistry or real entertainment.

Its prices shot up at the start of 2018 to reach a market cap of $5 billion. Ironically, this enormous increase was mostly due to its announcement of new corporate partnerships. TRON's dream of a decentralized Internet that is free of pure profit motivations might be a long way off, but there's no denying that the value of the coin is skyrocketing. In fact, the ICO was so popular, it broke the servers of Binance, the issuing website.

Since then, any discussion of Tron has been fraught with divisions. Some criticisms cite the lack of an actual product; others cite stolen code that has been worked into its release.

How does TRON work?

TRON is all about creating a social-user ecosystem centered on content creation and having creators interact directly with consumers. The idea is to cut out expensive intermediaries who take profits and sites that treat their users as fodder for advertisers.

It also uses the blockchain to add transparency to the idea of popularity. Rather than having manufactured superstars, it lets everyone see what's actually popular rather than just being pushed forward by record labels or other brands that manufacture celebrities.

It does this by putting a direct line between creators and consumers, while taking steps to ensure a lively and healthy ecosystem.

To this end, TRON developers have created a formula that determines creator rewards. This reward system takes into account the following:

- **Creation:** Simply creating content and thereby contributing to a healthy ecosystem is enough to earn rewards. Those wo make more regular contributors will obviously earn more rewards.

- **Popularity and engagement metrics:** Likes, shares, comments and other signals of frequent user engagement or enjoyment will increase the rewards provided to content creators.

It also plans to offer tools to facilitate content creation. One example is by letting developers use the platform to create games specially designed for TRON or by offering a range of new communication channels between users.

The TRX token is the native currency of the TRON ecosystem. TRON isn't mined in the traditional sense that we see it done with other cryptocurrencies. It will essentially be "mined" by content creators, with those who add their content to the network rewarded with new TRX based on the quality of content they produce. TRON's stated goals include becoming the following:

- A high-quality content hosting platform.

- A social network that provides a link among all users.

- A digital currency to bridge users.

- A payment network.

- An autonomous ecosystem.

TRX owners will also get voting rights on the platform's management and decision-making. The goal is to encourage people to hold TRX for the long run, which should help shore up the currency's value against inflation. TRON developers expect that the entire process will take about eight to ten years to achieve.

In mid-2018, TRON will go through its first major upgrade. The Exodus event will switch the platform over from its beta-phase using the Ethereum blockchain to its main, in-house TRON blockchain. The switch from the testnet to the mainnet will greatly reduce the fees and improve the scalability.

TRON's conundrum

As an idealistic project, TRON will inherently fail. Despite the promises of the blockchain, bringing the Internet's content under the TRON umbrella will only centralize it, rather than decentralize it.

And even if TRON does manage to accomplish its ambitious goals, will advertisers and existing media giants simply migrate over to TRON in order to keep capturing an audience? In practical terms, there's nothing inherently decentralized about TRON, despite its goals.

Some aspects of the reward algorithm are geared toward penalizing click-farming or other manipulation. But in truth there's no actual way to prevent native advertising, crowd manipulation or ugly mob mentality in the TRON ecosystem. At a glance, the entire project might have little to recommend it, but looking at it from a more mercenary angle shows a different view.

Despite all its talk of decentralization, TRON aims to become a centralized content creation tool, a hosting platform, a social media giant and a payment network all in one. This is an exceptionally lucrative and challenging business plan. TRON's idealism and talk of decentralization can be considered a branding exercise and a way of cushioning the impact from its ongoing development of corporate partnerships.

But is it enough? Functionally, TRON has little to offer other than a unique reward algorithm for content creation. Almost any cryptocurrency can offer similar transparency and be used by consumers to directly reward content creators. In fact, numerous platforms offering a more concise focus area are emerging.

If TRON succeeds, it will be based on the strength of its business chops and on its ability to disrupt the giant social media and online content platforms. If it succeeds, buying TRON today might be like buying cheap Facebook shares. If it doesn't succeed, then it will be about as useful as buying Dogecoin.

The TRON debate

Some supporters of TRON shoot back by saying the long-term vision of TRON is clearly set out in the whitepaper and that claims of plagiarized code are just fake news. Whatever the reality is, some of the wild price gains TRON has shown since its launch have made it an emotive topic. One of the strongest criticisms of the TRON project has been the unclear supply of the TRX tokens itself.

According to the TRON whitepaper, this pre-mined token is distributed according to certain "rules." Upon a closer look at the way TRON is distributed, the "rules" may just be values that the TRON development team made to ensure price control. The trouble with this is that if the claims of there being no actual product that TRON is developing are true, TRON could be a very elaborate scam.

There are 100 billion units of TRON as its whitepaper states. Of that 100 billion, 40% has been allotted for public offering, and 35% has been set aside for the "TRON foundation and ecosystems." Another 15% has been transferred to "private sale," plus a final 10% has been placed in "early payment of support to accompany me joy (Beijing) technology company, Ltd," which seems a little unprofessional from TRON's public face and creator Justin Sun.

Justin Sun is a Chinese national who received a Master's degree from the University of Pennsylvania after completing his Bachelor's degree at the prestigious Chinese university, Peking University. His achievements include founding a popular social media site Peiwo, which is believed to have been, or is now using, TRON's blockchain technology. Mr. Sun styles himself on the Tron website as being the protégé of Jack Ma, one of the most influential tech tycoons in China and the world having founded Alibaba.

That relationship is important. The reason for this is that there have been reports of senior technical staff of Alibaba being recruited to TRON laboratories. Regardless of whether these developments lead to a sound technical product, it certainly adds to the hype surrounding TRON. In addition to that, Mr. Sun has also been named twice in Forbes' promising global entrepreneurs under 30 list.

The reaction to the TRON ICO was promising. That is true even considering the turbulent conditions the TRON ICO saw at the time. In August of 2017, just as TRON was entering the ICO phase, the People's Bank of China issued regulations banning all ICOs in China. In spite of this, the Tron ICO still took place on August 28, 2017.

From this point on, having a clear picture of exactly who has how much TRX becomes difficult. Available information shows the first TRX transaction, otherwise known as the genesis block, being deposited to a certain wallet. As late as 19 December 2017, transactions have drawn the total held by that wallet to around 85 million TRX, which represents exactly 0.085% of all TRX issued.

The three largest transactions - which were roughly 10 billion, 15 billion and 16 billion - were moved to three different wallets (called wallet set A). Wallet set A then moved those tokens to different wallets (called wallet set B) all on 1 Oct 2017, exactly 29 minutes apart. The total of those three largest transactions equaled well over 41% of all TRX issued.

It is important to have a look at the average transaction for wallet set B. This is because the average transaction amount tends to be around 350 million TRX. This could be important because it could suggest that whoever is in control of the three wallet set B wallets could be creating artificial liquidity. That means that there could be a manufactured liquidity, which would signal that the price of TRX is being manipulated in a very controlled way.

Without access to advanced cryptographic tools, these suggestions are just speculation. However, at first glance, there is a pattern of very controlled TRX movement that clearly originates from the genesis block. The "rules" the TRON whitepaper references concerning the distribution of TRX are thrown into disarray by this idea.

It should be recalled that 60% of TRX was to be held by Tron's development teams and other organizations associated with TRON. The other 40% was for public sale. It is possible that the 41% of TRX that was moved to wallet set B could be in public hands. It is also possible that maybe only a very small fraction of that 41% is in wallets that have nothing to do with TRON. What this means is that only Justin Sun has the best understanding of exactly how much TRX is in whose hands.

What these numbers demonstrate more than anything else is the extent to which good marketing will have on a trader's understanding of an ICO. In this case, TRON has a questionable future regarding whether its innovations will be globally successful or not. That does not seem to deter a large body of people who believe that the TRON vision will deliver. The trouble is that there are still a lot of questions to be answered. One of those questions is whether the price of TRX is subject to price manipulation.

TRON price prediction

With all of that in mind, what should impact the price of TRON in the future?

Here is what could drive TRON's growth?

- **Partnerships:** TRON has secured partnerships with a number of big names in the content entertainment industry, including Uplive, Bitmain, Game.com, BitGuild and bike sharing system, oBike. These could help drive the popularity and growth of the platform plus potentially lead to future arrangements with other corporate partners. Partnership announcements have also previously affected the price of TRX in a significant way.

- **Justin Sun:** TRON founder Justin Sun has been listed in the Forbes "30 Under 30" list and previously founded China's Snapchat competitor Peiwo. Sun also has a large public profile and is reported to enjoy close ties with Jack Ma, the founder of Chinese ecommerce behemoth Alibaba. Sun's frequent activity through channels like Twitter has become almost legendary, frequently impacting the price of TRX.

- **Speculation:** From December 9, 2017, to January 9, 2018, the price of TRX rose a whopping 3,650%. There were several factors behind the spike, but such rapid growth could potentially attract speculators and those affected by FOMO (fear of missing out) looking to take advantage of any future price hikes.

- **Mainnet launch:** TRON's Exodus launch will see it move from its testing phase (think of it like a beta program) to its final TRON blockchain (termed a mainnet). This is expected to launch by May 31, 2018. (If you read this book after that date, simply check the finder website for news.) Exodus aims to offer negligible fees and increased scalability and will see TRON switch from the Ethereum network to its own platform.

- **Potential:** TRON's aim is to create a platform where users can freely publish, store and own data. The plan is to cut out middlemen, such as the Apple Store and Google Play, giving ownership back to content creators.

And what could hold TRON back?

- **No working product:** As of April 2018, TRON does not have a working product. Until the mainnet is released, there is bound to be a great deal of uncertainty surrounding the platform's viability.

- **Justin Sun:** Some critics have pointed to TRON's over-reliance on Sun for marketing and networking as a potential drawback. If Sun's credibility is brought into question, for example by the plagiarism scandal mentioned below, or if he decides to move his focus on to other projects, this could have a big impact on the public perception of TRON.

- **Questionable marketing:** TRON has been criticized in the past for making misleading announcements about corporate partnerships. For example, in January 2018, it was accused of using "creative marketing" to over-hype its partnership with Chinese firm Baofeng.

- **Plagiarism accusations:** In January 2018, TRON was hit by explosive allegations that sections of its whitepaper were plagiarized from Filecoin and IPFS. Though Justin Sun responded with a tweet claiming the lack of referencing (and other whitepaper issues) was due to a translation error, the news had a big impact on the overall public perception of the project.

- **Lack of adoption:** Another key factor determining the value of TRX will be whether the platform can achieve widespread adoption. It will need to compete with established content channels such as Facebook, Instagram and Google Play as well as blockchain platforms like LBRY and Po.et.

- **TRX distribution:** Some commentators have questioned whether a large portion of TRX tokens are controlled by a small number of users, allowing market manipulation of the TRX price.

What's coming up in TRON's roadmap?

Upcoming developments and upgrades are also key considerations when attempting to forecast future TRX price fluctuations. Of course, the biggest upcoming development in TRON's roadmap is the launch of its mainnet, which has been brought forward to May 31, 2018. Known as Exodus, this will see TRON launch its free platform for data publication, storage and dissemination.

Considering the criticism that's been levelled at TRON for its lack of a working product, the mainnet launch will be watched with considerable interest by TRX holders. In fact, the entire market will be watching.

It's also important to point out that Exodus is just the first of six phases in TRON's development. Odyssey, Great Voyage, Apollo, Star Trek and Eternity are all phases still to come, with the last of these scheduled for completion around 2027. It's worth researching these phases if you want a better idea of TRON's long-term plans.

TRON's competition

The value of TRX in the months and years ahead will in part be influenced by how TRON compares to other competitors in the online entertainment content marketplace. Key competitors to keep an eye on include the following:

- **Established content platforms:** Facebook, Twitter, Amazon, Instagram, Apple iTunes and Google Play are just some of the big names that currently control the lion's share of the market. None of these platforms will relinquish their audiences without a big and expensive fight, so the onus will be on TRON to position itself as a viable alternative.

- **LBRY:** With an aim to overcome censorship and centralized control, LBRY is a community-run digital media library and marketplace where creators can upload their content. They are able to set their own terms and fees about how their content is shared.

- **Po.et:** This is another blockchain platform where publishers and creators can manage their digital media assets, Po.et aims to provide incontrovertible proof of ownership and simplify the attribution process.

- **SingularDTV:** SingularDTV is a blockchain platform designed to provide artists and creators with a system where they can build, monetize, manage and distribute their various projects.

Beyond 2018: What does the future hold for TRON?

What 2018 and the years that follow have in store for TRON will be greatly influenced by how well the launch of the TRON mainnet goes since it is a crucial milestone for the project. If the launch is successful and the platform runs as promised, it'll go a long way to silencing some of TRON's critics. Of course, the headlines will be markedly different if the mainnet is a flop.

The role of Justin Sun will also be crucial. Depending on who you ask, Sun is either as important and influential as Elon Musk is to Tesla or someone who plagiarizes whitepapers and engages in some questionable marketing practices. Whatever the case may be, there's no doubt that Sun has been a real driving force behind TRON's evolution so far.

Whether the project experiences future growth will come down to the battle for widespread adoption. The Internet giants that currently control most online entertainment content aren't just going to roll over and let a new arrival assume control of the market, so TRON's ability to position itself as a reliable and popular platform will be vital.

So while the future for TRON is quite uncertain at the moment, we can expect the picture to become much clearer through 2018. In the meantime, supporters will be hoping Justin Sun and the project as a whole can avoid courting any more controversy.

For a full comparison of the exchanges that allow you to purchase TRON (TRX), check the finder website.

XX. TECHNICAL ANALYSIS

If you're new to the cryptocurrency market and the trading market in general, then you can easily get overwhelmed by the way information is presented. Many exchanges and websites will provide detailed graphs alongside their price charts and price predictions, analyzing the way the market is behaving. While the glossary at the end of this book can help you wade through the technical jargon, it's worth diving a little deeper into what these graphs are showing, so you can monitor the rise and fall of your cryptocurrencies more accurately.

What is a technical analysis?

A technical analysis is an overarching term used when you take existing, real-world data from the cryptocurrency market and attempt to plot it forward in the hope of predicting where it will go next. It's a prediction, not a forecast. In the best case scenario, this allows you to forecast when the market will be bearish (trending down) or bullish (trending up). If predicted correctly, this allows you to buy when the market price is low (buying on the dip) and sell when it is high in order to make a profit.

As this is the desire of the majority of traders, we often see natural corrections in prices over short periods that don't disrupt the overall trends seen in long periods. If the market is bullish for a substantial amount of time, demand will reduce the supply of coins for sale and the price will increase. As the price goes up, you can expect it to become bearish at some point as people try to capitalize by selling their coins. As they sell, supply begins to outweigh demand, causing the price to go down.

These course corrections can happen within days, if not hours, and are what day traders look for in order to make a profit. However, those looking for longer term wins will look at longer periods – weeks, months or years – in search of useful guidance on general upward or downward trends. It prevents you from selling off in a panic at a downturn in price that may actually be just a natural correction to a period of upward price rise.

Doing a technical analysis of a coin helps you read the market. It involves examining price charts and graphs in different ways, and looking to find a consensus within that information to help you predict where the market is going. In this chapter, we're going to go through the most common elements you will see on a chart and explain how they work, what they are telling you and how they intersect with each other.

Before diving in, it is also important to remember that you cannot know for sure what will happen in the future. A technical analysis uses what has already happened to attempt to forecast what will happen in the future, but nothing is certain. You cannot predict what will happen in the future: especially with the cryptocurrency market, where the media, influencers, whales (rich traders who can buy/sell large volumes) and governments can have such a sudden and significant impact on price.

Instead of predicting then, a technical analysis allows you to go into the future day(s) of trading as best prepared as possible.

How does a candlestick work?

One of the first head scratching moments you are likely to come across when you begin exploring price charts is the candlestick. These are the rectangle shaped objects on a chart colored either green or red/pink, with lines coming out of the bottom and top. The rectangle shape with the line out of the top resembles a candlestick – hence the name. But what is a candlestick telling you?

The rectangle itself shows the gap between the opening and closing balance for that coin during the period you are searching. So if you are looking at the price of a coin by day, then the colored rectangular part of each candlestick is showing you the difference between the opening balance for that day's trading and the closing balance. If the candlestick is green, the bottom of that rectangle shows the opening price, and the top the closing price. Green is good because it means that the value of your coin increased during that day.

If the candlestick is reddish in color, it means the opening price is at the top, and the closing price is at the bottom. This is obviously bad news as it means that the value of your coin went down during the day. However, there is more to the story.

The "wicks" that come out of the rectangle on the top and bottom show the highest and lowest range of prices within that day. For example, during any 24-hour period, a coin may have opened at $1 and closed at $2. However, at some point during the day it may have dipped as low as 50c and risen as high as $3. This is useful information, as it shows just how volatile the market is within each single 24-hour period, and not just the final opening and closing prices.

The more volatile the market, the higher the chance that the gain (or loss) your coin suffered over the course of the day may continue or be corrected on the next trading day. This is because it shows if the market is expanding down more than it is expanding up or vice versa. It can also show whether the market is consolidating. This information can give you an indication as to whether a coin is likely to crash or moon.

Imagine a scenario where the wick at the top of the candle is very short. This would suggest that the coin is on the up as it has closed the day close to its highest recorded price for the day. If the wick at the top was long, it would show that, at some point during the day, the price of the coin was much higher, but people started to sell it to make a profit. This would suggest the market is about to go down or go bearish.

Conversely, if the wick at the bottom of a candle is short, it suggests that people are still selling the coin. This adds to the supply and suggests the price is likely to go down even further. However, if the wick at the bottom is quite long, then it suggests the price of the coin has already dipped, and people have started buying it again hoping to get it at its lowest value. This may result in an upward movement on the following day.

Understanding Volume

Another metric you will see when looking at price graphs is the volume. There are two types of volume to consider. There is the literal volume of sales, which is how many coins were traded in the period you are looking at (daily, weekly, monthly, etc.), and then there is the dollar volume for that period.

The literal volume, the amount of coins traded, often appears as a column along the bottom of a price chart. The height of this column acts as a visual identifier of the volume, and the color indicates if that volume tended to be more bearish (sales) or bullish (buys). Volume is important in that it shows just how serious a bullish or bearish market is. The larger the volume of trade, the bigger the volatility we'll see in the price. Traders like volatility because it provides the opportunity to buy at a low price and sell on a high price.

If we're looking to predict whether a bullish or bearish trend will continue over an extended period, the volume can act as an indicator. If the volume of trades is high and the price is increasing, then there is some genuine momentum in this price swing. So if you were thinking of selling your coin, you may want to hold off with the expectation that the upward trend will continue and possibly even buy more in anticipation of that rise.

Of course, you should never look at just one indicator. You should look at patterns that align across a number of indicators. So what you may be looking for then is not only a large spike in the volume of transactions, but to see it combined with a long wick at the top of the candlestick. Why? This indicates that the bulls are no longer driving the price upwards, and the bears have taken control and are starting a downward trend. In which case, it could be a good time to sell.

If volume of trades overall is low, then it would suggest that there isn't much conviction in the market, so that any change we see in price (upwards or downwards) is less likely to continue into the next period.

If you notice a sudden, big spike in volume, which may occur around a big announcement, pay special attention. It likely indicates that there is about to be some significant movement in that coin's price up or down. This can provide the heads-up you need to buy or sell before the larger market gets wind that something is happening.

As for the second type of volume, the dollar volume for a given period, that relates to the price of the coin multiplied by the volume traded. This allows us to compare coins across different prices. For example, a spike of a million trades in a coin worth $1 may sound like a lot, but only $1 million dollars' worth of trading has been done. But a spike of 100,000 trades of a $100 coin is actually far more explosive as this shows $100 million dollars' worth of trading has been done. The latter coin, while doing less literal volume, is actually more significant of a change if you were deciding between the two.

Moving Averages

While looking for volume and candlestick trends over short periods is a vital part of predicting price movements, it's dangerous to consider just these metrics. You want to also look at the price movements across a larger section of time (days, weeks, months, etc.) to ensure you don't get tricked by the market into selling or buying at the wrong time. This is where the moving average comes into play.

There are two types of moving average you will come across while examining price graphs: the SMA (Simple Moving Average) and the EMA (Exponential Moving Average).

The SMA is, as its name suggests, quite simple. It displays the average closing price over a set period of time. Let's say you are looking at a seven-day period. The SMA value for any day is that day, plus the previous six days, divided by seven. This line moves up and down across your graph because each day sees a new closing price added and an older closing price dropped. This is why it's considered a moving average. The SMA helps show a trend over time on a market, taking out all the volatility within a 24-hour period and instead taking a bird's eye view of the landscape.

The way you would see these lines indicated on a chart are SMA(7) or MA(7). The SMA/MA is self-explanatory while the number in the brackets represents the number of periods the average is taking into account. If you are looking at a daily chart then that is seven days. If it is an hourly chart, it is seven hours.

The EMA is a slightly different beast and more complicated to explain. Using the seven-day example from above, rather than treating the closing balance of each day equally (and just dividing the total sum by seven), the EMA graph weights each day differently based on its proximity to the current day. So the previous day is given more weight than the day before it, with descending importance granted to days as you go back through the seven-day period. The EMA is more reactionary and can adapt quicker to volatility in the market.

So how does a moving average help you read the cryptocurrency market? It shows the support or resistance to buying or selling at a certain price point. If the closing price for the day gets up past the moving average, it lends support to the idea that it is a bullish market and you should look for an opportunity to sell. If the closing price dips below the moving average, it suggests that the market is moving into a period of downward trend and that we may start to see some buying.

A rule of thumb when dealing with moving averages is that the longer the period examined, the stronger the indicator. With that in mind, our example of seven days isn't that strong. Looking at 70 days would provide a more robust indication of whether the market is beginning to move above or below the moving average.

One of the reasons why this form of technical analysis is quite effective is because traders use them to set buy and sell limits on coins. Buy and sell limits are pre-determined smart contracts set up within an exchange, whereby a trader says they will buy (or sell) a coin when the price hits a certain figure. As it is a smart contract, it will activate automatically, without human intervention, when the correct figure is reached.

For example, imagine that the price of a coin is at $10, and the moving average is $15. A trader may create a smart contract with an exchange that stipulates a purchase of 100 coins when the price hits $15. This is because a movement like this would suggest a bullish market and a likely price increase beyond that. Conversely, if the price of the coin then rose to $20, the moving average would rise with it, perhaps getting to $17. At this point, the trader may set a sell limit of $17, whereby those 100 coins will be sold if the market shows a bearish trend and dips back below the moving average.

In this scenario, the trader has used the moving average as a guide to hopefully make a minimum profit of $2 per coin.

Ultimately what you are trying to do with a moving average is predict where the market has set its buy and sell limits. Experimenting with different moving average periods and comparing them to candlesticks is key. If you can see the wicks on candles are extending above or below the moving average (depending on which side of the line the price is at), but the closing balance is not passing the line, you're seeing an indication of support (above the line) or resistance (below the line) for that price. This is because as soon as the market went past that point, smart contracts were activated, bringing the price back.

This gives you some indication of where the buy and sell limits of the market have been set.

Deciding whether you should use SMAs or EMAs depends on the type of trading you want to do. Generally, SMAs are more useful if you are trading in longer periods of time, say weekly or even daily, as it doesn't react to volatility and gives a more wide-angled view of the market. For day traders who are looking at hourly (or less) changes, the EMA can more quickly spot price fluctuations and opportunities to make money.

How to trade with the trend

Using the above information as your weapon, you can now begin to look at larger scale trends. This is best defined by the wicks on the end of our candlesticks. When looking at a price graph, you will be able to note the lowest candlestick wick in that period. This shows the lowest point during that period at which the coin was traded. Let's call that Point A.

Now look at the days since that initial date. As long as the low point, the bottom of the bottom wick, on a given day is higher than Point A, the market is in an upward trend. You'll often need to look at months or even years' worth of data to see if there is an upward trend as the market will naturally consolidate and fluctuate in waves in shorter periods (days or weeks). But in general, if those low wicks continue to be higher than Point A, you're in an upward trend.

Naturally, the converse situation is a downward trend. If you have, over your long period view, a clear high point, which we'll call Point B, and the top of the top wick is consistently lower than Point B in the days that follow, you have a downward trend.

Trading with the trend means you are buying on the up and selling on the down. This is the overall goal for those looking towards longer term gains with their coin purchases.

When you're looking to establish a trend line on a graph, you will click two points – the point where you are starting your trend (the lowest or highest) and the current day. However, to be sure that a trend is indeed a trend, you want to see at least one of the candlesticks in between these points touch the line. This third touch makes the trend line valid; if you can't get that, then the period isn't giving you clear evidence of a trend. And if you can get more than three touches, then you're increasing the validity of that trend.

It's important to note that trends can be deceptive. Something that looks clearly like a downtrend in a 90-day period may, when you zoom out to a 900-day period, show itself to be a consolidation period in a grander upward trend. So make sure you're aware when you analyze for trends that if you look at the 90-day trend without looking at the 900-day trend, you could get caught out.

What is the RSI (Relative Strength Index)?

We've now taken you through the nuts and bolts of reading the price chart on your favorite exchange or website, but there is plenty more on offer. As you can imagine, there are multiple ways of visualizing this data and interpreting the mathematics. These various visualizations are called indicators, and their main motive is to help you arrive at a forecast of what may happen in the future quicker and with more confidence.

Remember, a technical analysis only describes what has happened in the past to offer a suggestion of what might happen in the future. It does not predict what will happen!

One of the more popular indicators you will come across is the Relative Strength Index, or RSI. The RSI looks at the momentum in a coin's trading history to try and predict whether it is overbought or oversold. It's represented by a scale of 0 to 100 (with 100 being the overbought end) and looks back over 14 periods in establishing its number.

The relative strength index is established by looking at the average gains over a 14-day period, divided by the average losses. It's a moving indicator, so each new day is a new 14-day period since the oldest day drops out and the most recent day pops in.

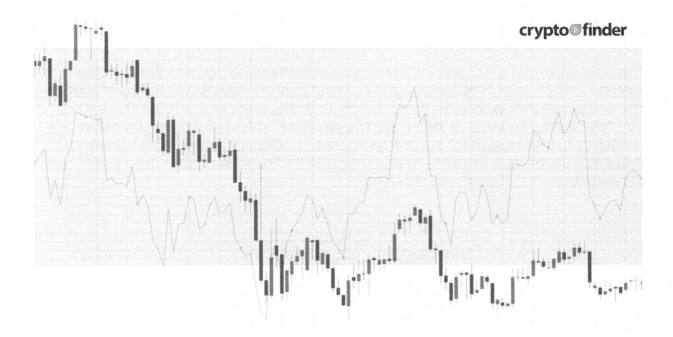

A coin becomes overbought if there is an extended period of gains, and it is oversold if there is an extended period of losses. What this tells us is that the market will be ready for a natural correction at the extremes of the RSI. Generally, a coin is considered to be overbought if the RSI is past 70, and oversold if it is below 30. If, as part of your technical analysis, you see the RSI is into either of these extremes, it adds to the argument that there is about to be a reversal in the market.

If volumes, candlesticks and moving averages also support this argument, you can more confidently buy or sell.

Explaining Inside Bars

We can also use candlesticks to look for consolidation and tightening of the market. Let's say we are looking at a daily chart. If a candlestick one day, including its wicks, is smaller than the day before and fits within its range, it is called an inside bar. It shows that the market is consolidating. So if one day a coin reached a high of $10 and a low of $5, and then the next day it reached a high of $8 and a low of $6, it is an inside bar. (It is within the $10 to $5 range of its predecessor.)

If the next day you then got a high of $7 and a low of $6.50, you have a second consecutive day of inside bars. This shows that the market is tightening up. This is important to note as, historically, a tightening market is an indicator that a breakout is about to occur in the near future. A breakout is a spike in trading volume, driving the price quickly and significantly either down or up. It occurs when the market has tightened to a point where traders aren't making money, so the situation becomes delicately poised. When a move is made either way, it then tends to be big.

If you are looking at the charts and notice a period of tightening or consolidation, then you may be seeing the seeds of a breakout. This could go on for days. But at the point at which the next candlestick exceeds its predecessors range and is not an inside bar, this is when you can expect a breakout. If the candlestick exceeds the high point of the day before, it will be a bullish breakout; if it dips beyond the low point, it will be a bearish breakout. If this movement is backed up by a large change in trading volume, you have a good indicator that a significant price shift is on.

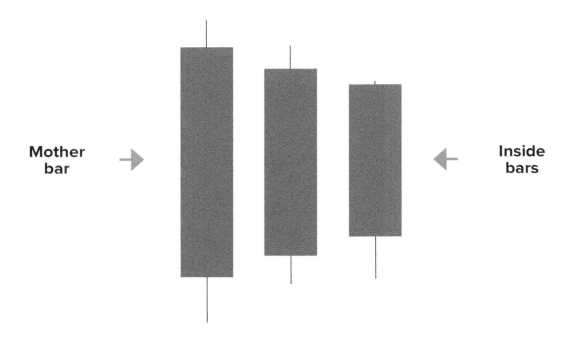

What is Arbitrage?

For the majority of this chapter we have explored the price chart since it is the most common way to read the market; however, it is not the only way. More common than a price chart is the price table. It shows a list of all the coins, shows whether they are going up or down, and what the high points and low points are for the day.

More importantly, you may also see what the prices of a coin are on different exchanges. For example, you might see that one exchange could be buying a coin at $2.10, while another is selling the same coin at $1.90.

Simple math should tell you that if you go to the second exchange and buy coins at $1.90, then go to the first exchange and sell them at $2.10, there is a solid 20 cent profit to be made. This situation, a difference in the price of a cryptocurrency between two exchanges at the same time, is called arbitrage. For the eagle-eyed trader with the capacity to swiftly act with their trades, it can be an opportunity to make some money.

However, there are caveats to consider. There are fees charged by exchanges for making these transactions, plus, the need for a transaction to be confirmed on the blockchain can delay the process long enough for the window of opportunity to close before it is executed. These are just two factors to consider and take into account before you pounce on an arbitrage opportunity.

XXI. HOW TO STAY UP TO DATE

Few industries move as fast, and are as volatile, as the cryptocurrency market. As much as this book arms you with everything you need to know to confidently step into this world, you'll want to stay up-to-date with the latest news and prices if you are going to buy wisely. Finder is an independent comparison site that not only provides the latest news, but real-time cryptocurrency prices and reviews of the wallets and exchanges you'll need to get started. We also offer exclusive interview and video content, as well as podcasts and price predications, all focused on cryptocurrency.

Finder is a global company, with country-specific websites. However, the cryptocurrency market knows no boundaries. As a result, almost all the information you will find across the finder websites will be relevant to you. The only significant information that is regionally specific is content about converting local fiat money for a cryptocurrency.

As well as visiting the finder website daily and watching our vide content on cryprtofinder. tv, you can also sign-up to a newsletter for a wrap-up delivered right to your inbox, and follow our social media platforms. If you have any questions, don't hesitate to ask in the comments section of the website and you'll be answered as soon as possible. We have journalists covering the industry from all over the world. Best of luck on your cryptocurrency journey!

USA/Global site = www.finder.com/cryptocurrency

Australian site = www.finder.com.au/cryptocurrency

UK site = www.finder.com/uk/cryptocurrency

New Zealand Site = www.finder.com/nz/cryptocurrency

XXII. GLOSSARY OF TERMS

To help ease you into the cryptocurrency landscape, Finder has created the ultimate cryptocurrency glossary. This not only gives you an overview of the terms used day-to-day in the cryptocurrency world, but goes deeper to explain their importance and where they fit into the conversation.

51% Attack: If more than half the computer power on a network is run by a single person or a single group of people, then a 51% attack is in operation. This means the person or group has full control of the network and can negatively affect a cryptocurrency by halting mining, stopping or changing transactions and reusing coins.

Address: Every cryptocurrency coin has a unique address that identifies where it sits on the blockchain. This location is where the coin's ownership data is stored, and where any changes are registered when it is traded. These addresses differ in appearance between cryptocurrencies but are usually a string of over 30 characters.

Airdrop: A marketing campaign that refers to the expedited distribution of a cryptocurrency to a specific group of people. It usually occurs when the creator of a cryptocurrency provides their coin to low-ranked traders or existing community members in order to build their use and popularity. They are usually given away for free or in exchange for simple tasks like sharing news of the coin with friends.

Algorithm: Mathematic instructions coded into and implemented by computer software in order to produce a desired outcome.

All-Time High: The highest price ever achieved by a cryptocurrency.

All-Time Low: The lowest price ever achieved by a cryptocurrency.

Altcoins: Bitcoin was the first and is the most successful of all the cryptocurrencies. All the other coins are grouped together under the category or altcoins. Ether, for example, is an altcoin as is Ripple.

AML: Acronym for anti-money laundering.

Anti-Money Laundering Laws: These are a set of international laws that hope to prevent criminal organizations or individuals laundering money through cryptocurrencies into real-world cash.

Application Specific Integrated Circuit: A piece of computer hardware, similar to a graphics card or a CPU, which has been designed specifically to mine cryptocurrency. They are built specifically to efficiently solve hashing problems.

Arbitrage: There are many exchanges at any given time trading the same cryptocurrency, and they can do so at different rates. Arbitrage is the act of buying from one exchange and then selling it to the next exchange if there is a margin between the two that is profitable.

ASIC: Acronym for application specific integrated circuit.

ATH: Acronym for all-time high.

ATL: Acronym for all-time low.

Atomic Swap: A way of letting people directly and cost-effectively exchange one type of cryptocurrency for another, at current rates, without needing to buy or sell.

Bag: If you have a large quantity of units in a certain type of cryptocurrency, you'd have a bag of them.

Bear/Bearish: When the price of a cryptocurrency has a negative price movement.

Bear Trap: A trick played by a group of traders aimed at manipulating the price of a cryptocurrency. The bear trap is set by this group all selling their cryptocurrency at the same time, which bluffs the market into thinking there is a drop incoming. As a result, other traders sell their assets, which drives the price down further. Those who set the trap then buy back their assets, which are now at a lower price. The overall price then rebounds, allowing them to make a profit.

Bitcoin: The very first cryptocurrency. It was first created in 2008 by an individual or group of individuals operating under the name Satoshi Nakamoto. It was intended to be a peer-to-peer decentralized electronic cash system.

Block: The blockchain is made up of blocks. Each block holds a historical database of all cryptocurrency transactions made until the block is full. It's a permanent record, like a bag of data, which can be opened and viewed at any time.

Block Explorer: An online tool for exploring the blockchain of a cryptocurrency, which you can use to watch and follow live all the transactions happening on the blockchain. Block explorers can serve as a blockchain analysis and provide information such as total network hash rate, coin supply, transaction growth, etc.

Block Height: The number of blocks connected in the blockchain. For example, height 0, would be the very first block, which is also called the genesis block.

Block Reward: A form of incentive for the miner who successfully calculates the hash (verification) in a block. Verification of transactions on the blockchain generates new coins in the process, and the miner is rewarded a portion of these.

Blockchain: The blockchain is a digital ledger of all the transactions in a particular cryptocurrency ever made. It is composed of individual blocks (see definition above) that are chained to each other through a cryptographic signature. Each time a block's capacity is reached, a new block is added to the chain. The blockchain is repeatedly copied and saved onto thousands of computers all around the world and must always match each other. As there is no master copy stored in one location, it's considered decentralized.

BTFD: Acronym for "buy the f$%king dip."

Bull/Bullish: When the price of a cryptocurrency has a positive price movement.

Bulletproofs: An upgrade to the blockchain that seeks to ensure confidentiality in transactions by hiding the amount being transferred while still providing cryptographic proof that it occurred.

Burned: If a coin has been made unspendable, it is said to be burned.

Buy the F$%king Dip: A less than savory phrase used when you're (enthusiastically) telling someone a currency has dipped to a low value and should be bought.

Buy Wall: When a large limit order has been placed to buy a cryptocurrency when it reaches a certain value, then that is a buy wall (also called a buy limit). This can prevent a cryptocurrency from falling below that value as demand will likely outstrip supply when the order is executed.

CAP: Shorthand for market capitalization (see definition below).

Central Ledger: When a single entity has control of all financial records, it is considered to be a central ledger. This is how banks operate.

Chain Linking: Each cryptocurrency has its own blockchain – the digital ledger that stores all transaction records. Chain linking is the process that occurs if you transfer one cryptocurrency to another. This requires the transaction to be lodged in two separate blockchains, so they must link together to achieve the goal.

Cipher: The name given to the algorithm that encrypts and decrypts information.

Circulating Supply: The total number of cryptocurrency coins that are in the public tradable space is considered the circulating supply. Some coins can be locked, reserved or burned, therefore unavailable to public trading.

Cold Storage: A term used to describe a wallet that is held offline; namely a paper wallet or hardware wallet (see below).

Confirmed: When a transaction has been confirmed, it means it has been approved by the network and permanently appended to the blockchain.

Consensus: When a transaction is made, all nodes on the network verify that it is valid on the blockchain and if so, they have a consensus.

Consensus Process: Refers to those nodes that are responsible for maintaining the blockchain ledger so that a consensus can be reached when a transaction is made. This is what miners do.

Consortium blockchain: This is a privately owned and operated, yet transparent to the public, blockchain.

Cryptocurrency: A form of money that exists as encrypted, digital information. Operating independently of any banks, a cryptocurrency uses sophisticated mathematics to regulate the creation and transfer of funds between entities.

Cryptographic Hash Function: This process happens on a node and involves converting an input, such as a transaction, into a fixed, encrypted alphanumeric string that registers its place in the blockchain. This conversion is controlled by a hashing algorithm, which is different for each cryptocurrency.

Cryptography: The process of encrypting and decrypting information.

DAO: Acronym for decentralized autonomous organization.

Dapp: Shorthand for decentralized application.

Decentralized Application: A computer program that utilizes a blockchain for data storage, runs autonomously, is not controlled or operated from a single entity and is open source. Also, its use is incentivized by the reward of fees or tokens.

Decentralized Autonomous Organization: Refers to organizations that are run by an application (computer program), rather than direct human input. Control of this application is granted to everyone, rather than a single central entity.

Decryption: Turning encrypted cipher text back into plain text.

Deflation: When the demand for a particular cryptocurrency decreases, bringing down the price of its economy.

Depth Chart: This graph plots the requests to buy (known as bids) and sell (known as asks) on a chart. Because you can put a limit order on your buy or sell transaction, the depth chart shows the crossover point at which the market is most likely to accept a transaction in a timely fashion. It also shows any significant buy walls or sell walls in play.

Deterministic Wallet: This type of wallet is created by producing multiple keys from a seed. If you lose this wallet, your wallet key can be recovered from the seed. Plus, when you make transactions, instead of producing new keys each time, you use variations from the seed, which makes it more transferable and easier to store.

Difficulty: When someone refers to difficulty in the cryptocurrency space, they are referring to the cost of mining in that moment in time. The more transactions that are trying to be confirmed at any single moment in time divided by the total power of the nodes on the network at that time determines the difficulty. The higher the difficulty, the greater the transaction fee – this is a fluid measurement that moves over time.

Digital Commodity: An intangible, hard-to-get asset that is transferred electronically and has a certain value.

Digital Currency: Another term for digital commodity

Digital Signature: Used to confirm that a document being transmitted electronically is authentic. They generally appear as a code generated by a public key encryption.

Distributed Ledger: A ledger that is stored in multiple locations so that any entries can be accessed and checked by multiple parties. In cryptocurrency, this refers to the blockchain being held on multiple nodes on the network, all of which are checked simultaneously.

Double Spend: This occurs when someone tries to send a cryptocurrency to two different wallets or locations at the same time.

Dump: The term used to describe selling all (or a lot) of your cryptocurrency.

Dumping: When many people dump at once, causing a sharp downward price movement.

Dust Transaction: People may look to slow the network by deliberately flooding it with minor transactions . These minuscule amounts are referred to as dust transactions.

DYOR: Acronym for do your own research.

Encryption: Converting plain text into unintelligible text with the use of a cipher.

ERC: Stands for Ethereum request for comments. It is a summation of proposed improvements to the Ethereum system.

ERC20: The standard to which each Ethereum token complies. It defines the way that each token behaves so that transactions are predictable. Other cryptocurrencies also use the ERC20 standard, piggybacking on the Ethereum network in the process.

Escrow: When an intermediary is used to hold the funds during a transaction, those funds are being held in escrow. This is usually undertaken by a third-party between the entity sending and the one receiving.

Ethereum: One of the top three cryptocurrencies in the world based on its market capitalization. Despite being open source and based on blockchain technology, it differs from bitcoin in two key ways: it allows developers to create dapps and also allows them to write smart contracts.

Ethereum Virtual Machine: A virtual machine that is effectively sitting in the cloud, which is Turing complete and is used by all nodes on the network during blockchain confirmations. It allows those on the node to execute random EVM Byte Code, which is a key part of the Ethereum Protocol.

EVM: Stands for Ethereum Virtual Machine.

Exchange: The platform through which cryptocurrencies are exchanged with each other, with fiat currencies and between entities. Exchanges can vary widely on the currency conversions they will enable and their fee structures.

FA: Acronym for fundamental analysis.

Faucet: If you find a website that offers to give you free cryptocurrency for connecting with them, it is termed a faucet. The majority of these are scams.

Fiat: Refers to money recognized as legal tender by governments, such as the US dollar, pound, euro and Australian dollar.

FOMO: An acronym for fear of missing out.Fork: When a new version of a blockchain is created, resulting in two versions of the blockchain running side-by-side, it is termed a fork. As a single blockchain forks into two, they will both run on the same network. Forks are categorized into two categories: soft or hard.

Frictionless: If there is no transaction cost and no restraints on trading, then the system is considered frictionless.

FUD: Acronym for fear, uncertainty and doubt.

Full Node: Some nodes download a blockchain's entire history in order to enforce its rules completely. As they fully enforce the rules, they are considered a full node.

Fundamental Analysis: A method through which you can attach value to a coin by looking at similar economic and financial factors and by researching the underlying motives of the creators and market opinion.

Futures Contract: This is a pre-approved contract between two entities to fulfill a transaction when the value of cryptocurrency hits a certain price. It's different from a limit order in that the buyer and seller are already nominated and bound. A futures contract becomes relevant when a buyer wants to go short and a seller wants to go long on the asset.

Gas: Gas is a measurement given to an operation in the Ethereum network that relates to the computational power required to complete it. That measurement relates to the fee offered to miners who process that transaction. Other operations have a small cost of 3 to 10 gas, but a full transaction costs 21,000 gas.

Gas Limit: When a user makes a transaction in the Ethereum network, they set their gas limit, which is the most they are willing to pay as a fee for that transaction. If the transaction is going to cost more gas than what is offered, the transaction will not go through. If it costs less, the difference will be refunded.

Gas Price: The amount you are willing to pay for a transaction in the Ethereum network. If you want miners to process your transaction quickly, then you should offer a high price. Gas prices are usually denominated in Gwei.

Genesis Block: The first or first few blocks of a blockchain.

Group Mining: Another term used to describe a mining pool (see below).

Gwei: The denomination used in defining the cost of gas. So, for example, you can set a gas price of 20000 Gwei.

Halving: Every time miners approve transactions on the bitcoin blockchain, they earn bitcoin. As each block on the blockchain fills up with transactions, a certain amount of bitcoin enters the marketplace. However, the number of bitcoin that will ever be created is finite and locked at 21 million. In order to ensure this cap is kept, the amount of bitcoin earned by miners for filling one block is halved at the completion of that block. This is called halving. For the record, by the year 2140, all 21 million bitcoin will be in circulation.

Hard Cap: During an ICO, the creator can set a hard cap. This is the maximum amount the creator wants to raise. The ICO will stop offering coins once this figure is reached.

Hard Fork: A fork in the blockchain that converts transactions previously labeled invalid to valid, and vice versa. For this fork to work, all nodes on the network must upgrade to the newest protocol.

Hardware Wallet: A physical device, similar to a USB stick, which stores cryptocurrency in its encrypted form. This is considered the most secure way to hold cryptocurrency.

Hash: The shorthand for cryptographic hash function (see description above).

Hash Rate: Measurement of performance that reveals how many hashes per second your computer is capable of producing. Each hash is an attempt to find a block by creating a unique block candidate and testing it against the network.

Hashing Power: The hash rate of a computer, measured in kH/s, MH/s, GH/s, TH/s, PH/s or EH/s depending on the hashes per second being produced. 1,000 kH/s = 1 MH/s - 1,000 MH/s = 1 GH/s - and so forth.

HODL: Acronym for hold on for dear life.

ICO: Acronym for initial coin offering.

Initial Coin Offering: In order to raise funds, the creator of a cryptocurrency will put an initial batch of its coins up for purchase. This is an initial coin offering.

JOMO: Acronym for joy of missing out.

KYC: Acronym for know your customer. This refers to a financial institution's obligation to verify the identity of a customer in line with AML laws.

LAMBO: Shorthand for Lamborghini, which is how someone might refer to themselves if they are getting rich quickly. The idea being, there is so much money coming in, they are going to go buy an exotic car.

Ledger: A record of financial transactions. A ledger cannot be changed; it can only be appended with new transactions.

Leverage: A loan of sorts, offered by a broker on an exchange during a process known as margin trading (see below).

Lightning Network: A peer-to-peer system for cryptocurrency micropayments that is focused on low latency and instant payments. They're typically low cost, scalable and can work across chains, and the transactions can be public or private.

Limit Order/Limit Buy/Limit Sell: If you set a rule whereby a cryptocurrency is sold or bought at a certain price, you are setting a limit order.

Liquidity: The liquidity of a cryptocurrency is defined by how easily it can be bought and sold without impacting the overall market price.

Locktime: If a transaction request comes with a rule delaying when it can be processed, such as until a set time arrives or until a certain block on the blockchain appears, that is referred to as the locktime.

Long: When you intend to take a large amount of cryptocurrency and stockpile it with the anticipation that it will grow in value, you are going long (or taking a long position).

MACD: Acronym for moving average convergence divergence.

Mainnet: The mainnet refers to the final version of a blockchain. During the beta-phase, the blockchain operates on what is called a testnet. It is possible for a cryptocurrency to be live and traded while still operating on its testnet ahead of a final migration across to the mainnet blockchain.

Margin Bear Position: This is the position you are taking if you are going "short."

Margin Bull Position: This is the position you are taking if you are going "long."

Market Capitalization: This is defined as the total number of coins in supply multiplied by the price. The cap = supply x price.

Margin Trading: A risky strategy used by experienced traders where they risk their existing coins to magnify the intensity of their trades. This allows them to buy more than they can afford using leverage provided by an exchange.

Market Order: As opposed to a limit order, a market order does not wait until a certain price to buy or sell; it does so at the price of the time the transaction order is made.

MCAP: Acronym for market capitalization.

Mining: The term, somewhat confusingly, given to the process of verifying transactions on a blockchain. In the process of solving the encryption challenges, the person donating the computer power is granted new fractions of the cryptocurrency.

Mining Contract: Instead of buying mining hardware, you rent out the hashing power of mining hardware for a certain amount of time. The renter does not pay for the hardware or the maintenance and electricity required to run it.

Mining Pool: If a number of miners combine their computing power together to try and help complete the transactions required to start a new block in the blockchain, they are in a mining pool. The rewards spread between those in the mining pool are proportionately based on the amount of power they contributed. The idea is that being in a mining pool allows for a better chance of successful hashing, and therefore getting enough cryptocurrency reward to have an income.

Money Services Business: A legal term that is used to represent an entity that transfers or converts money.

Moon: A term used to describe a major price movement upwards. For example, Ripple is going to the moon, or Ripple is mooning.

Moving Average Convergence Divergence: A part of doing a technical analysis of a cryptocurrency's value that tracks price-change momentum to try and forecast where a coin will go into the future.

MSB: Acronym for money services business.

Multipool Mining: If a miner moves from one cryptocurrency blockchain to another, depending on the profitability provided by the network at that moment in time, they are engaging in multipool mining.

Multisignature (Multisig Wallets): If in order for a transaction to go through, more than one user needs to provide their unique code, then it is multisignature. This system is set up at the creation of the account and is considered less susceptible to theft.

Network: A network refers to all the nodes committed to helping the operation of a blockchain at any given moment in time.

Node: Any computer that is connected to a blockchain's network, usually as miners, is referred to as a node.

Nonce: When a miner hashes a transaction, a random number is generated. This number is a nonce. The parameters from which that number is chosen changes based on the difficulty of the transaction.

OCO: Acronym for one cancels the other order.

One Cancels the Other Order: When two orders for cryptocurrency are placed simultaneously, with a rule in place whereby if one is accepted, the other is cancelled.

Oracles: The smart contracts stored on a blockchain are stuck within the network. They can only be reached by the external world through a program called an oracle. The oracle sends the data to and from the smart contract and the outside world as required. Oracles are most commonly found on the Ethereum network.

Overbought: If a large number of purchases of a specific cryptocurrency have been made, its price will increase for an extended period of time. At this juncture, it is considered overbought and a period of selling is expected.

Oversold: If a cryptocurrency has spent significant time being sold without an upward movement, it is considered oversold. In this condition, there would be concerns about whether it will bounce back.

Paper Wallet: Storing your wallet code (your private key) on a physical document makes it a paper wallet. It's also sometimes referred to as cold storage.

P2P: Acronym for peer to peer.

Peer to Peer: In a peer-to-peer connection, two or more computers network with each other without a centralized, third party being used as an intermediary.

PND: Acronym for pump and dump.

Pre-Sale: A period before an ICO goes public, where private traders or community members are able to buy the cryptocurrency.

Private Key: A string of numbers and letters that are used to access your wallet. While your wallet is represented by a public key, the private key is the password you should protect (with your life). You need your private key when selling or withdrawing cryptocurrencies since it acts as your digital signature.

Proof of Authority (PoA): A private key that gives the holder the right to create the blocks in a private blockchain. It can be held by a single entity or a set number of entities. This is an alternative to the proof-of-work model since instead of getting multiple random nodes to approve a transaction, a group of specific nodes that have been given the authority can approve the transaction. This is a far faster method.

Proof of Stake (PoS): Another alternative to proof of work, this caps the reward given to miners for providing their computational power to the network at that miner's holdings of that cryptocurrency. So if a miner holds three coins, they can only earn three coins. This system encourages miners to stick with a certain blockchain rather than converting their rewards to an alternate cryptocurrency.

Proof of Work (PoW): In order to receive a reward for mining a cryptocurrency, the miner must show that their computer contributed effort to approve a transaction. A variable is added to the process of hashing a transaction that demands that effort before a block can be successfully hashed. Having a hashed block proves the miner did work and deserves a reward – hence proof of work.

Protocols: The set of rules that defines how data is exchanged across a network.

Public Blockchain: A blockchain that can be accessed by any individual through a full node on their computer.

Public Key: This is your unique wallet address, which appears as a long string of numbers and letters. It is used to receive cryptocurrencies.

Pump: This is a term used to refer to an upward price movement, usually driven by whales pumping large sums of money into a cryptocurrency.

Pump and Dump: The frowned upon practice of buying a lot of one cryptocurrency to drive up its price, encouraging others to buy it as well and then selling the lot when there is a suitable margin.

REKT: Shorthand slang for "wrecked" and a term used to describe a bad loss in a trade.

Relative Strength Index: A type of technical analysis whereby you determine the momentum of a price change over time. It looks at recent changes in price exponentially, with the most recent changes given more weight than older ones. This produces an overall trend of movement for a cryptocurrency that can determine if the market is overbought (a reading higher than 70) or oversold (a reading lower than 30).

Ring Signature: A ring signature is a type of encryption process that retains anonymity for the user. The concept gives the network of nodes the power to approve a transaction on a blockchain without identifying which of the nodes requested the transaction. As a result, it cannot be traced.

RSI: Acronym for relative strength index.

Satoshi Nakamoto: The individual or group of individuals (it has never been confirmed) that created bitcoin.

Satoshi: This is the named used to describe the smallest unit of bitcoin. This figure is 0.00000001 BTC.

SATS: Another name for a Satoshi.

Scrypt: An algorithm that encrypts a key in such a fashion that it takes a serious amount of RAM to hash it. The system makes it challenging for hackers to attack. Despite its spelling, scrypt is pronounced "ess-crypt."

Seed: The origin point from which you created your wallet ID. Usually, a seed is a phrase or a series of words that can be used to regenerate your wallet ID if you lose it. It's something to keep very secret.

Segregated Witness: This is the name of the process of separating digital signature data from transaction data. This lets more transactions fit onto one block in the blockchain, improving transaction speeds.

SegWit: Acronym for segregated witness.

Selfish Mining: If a miner finds or creates a new block in the blockchain, and then doesn't share that information with the network, they are partaking in selfish mining. This is because other miners are now burning their computational power on an old block, allowing the selfish miner to get a head start on the new block.

Sell Wall: When a large limit order has been placed to sell when a cryptocurrency reaches a certain value, then that is a sell wall (or sell limit). This can prevent a cryptocurrency from rising above that value as supply will likely outstrip demand when the order is executed.

SHA-256: The name of the cryptographic hash function (the hashing algorithm) used by bitcoin. It's been subsequently used by a number of altcoins, too.

Sharding: Sharding is a way of splitting up the full blockchain history so each full node doesn't need the whole copy of it. It's considered a scaling solution for blockchains because as they grow larger, it begins to slow the network performance if every node is required to carry the full blockchain.

Shit Coin: No points for guessing this one. It's a term used to describe a cryptocurrency that is not expected to have a positive future.

Short: Also known as short selling, this is a concept whereby traders sell an asset they don't have when it is at a low price. The hope is that selling it will further drive the price down. They can then buy the asset at an even lower price than which they sold it to complete the deal. Thereby they earn a margin in the interim.

Smart Contracts: When a contract is written in computer code, as opposed to traditional legal language, it is deemed a smart contract. This programmed contract is set up to execute and carry itself out automatically under specified conditions. When a smart contract is on the blockchain, both parties can check its programming before agreeing to it, and then let it do its thing, confident it cannot be tampered with or changed. It lets two parties agree to complex terms without needing to trust each other and without involving any third parties. This functionality is the defining feature of the Ethereum blockchain.

Soft Fork: A fork in a blockchain protocol where previously valid transactions become invalid if they don't comply with the new rules. A soft fork is backwards-compatible, as the old nodes running the old protocol – those that did not follow the fork - will still consider new transactions on the forked path valid, rather than disregarding them. For a soft fork to work, a majority of the miners powering the network need to upgrade to the new protocol.

Software Wallet: A common form of wallet where the private key for an individual is stored within software files on a computer. This is the system you are likely to use if you sign up to an online wallet that is not associated with an exchange.

Solidity: A programming language similar to JavaScript, but focused on developing smart contracts. It's exported as bytecode, which is used by the Ethereum Virtual Machine that runs the Ethereum network.

TA: Acronym for technical analysis.

Technical Analysis: Using a trading tool to look at historical data on a cryptocurrency in the hope of forecasting its future.

Testnet: When a cryptocurrency creator is testing out a new version of a blockchain, the creator does so on a testnet. This runs like a second version of the blockchain, but doesn't impact the value associated with the primary, active blockchain.

Timestamp: The moment in time when a transaction was encrypted and regarded as proof that the data compiled in that transaction existed.

Token: If the coin of a cryptocurrencyrepresents a digital asset – as opposed to payment - it is referred to as a a token. Effectively, it's the digital code defining each fraction, which can be owned, bought and sold.

Tokenless Ledger: When a distributed ledger exists but doesn't need a currency in which to operate. With these blockchains, the miners upholding the network typically don't get a reward or payment.

TOR: Acronym for terms of reference.

Transaction: The value of cryptocurrency if moved from one entity to another on a blockchain network.

Transaction Fee: Usually very small fees given to the miners involved in successfully approving a transaction on the blockchain. This fee can vary depending on the difficulty involved in a transaction and overall network capabilities at that moment in time. If an exchange is involved in facilitating that transaction, they could take a cut of the overall transaction fee as well.

Turing Completeness: If a machine is capable of performing all conceivable programmable calculations, then it is Turing complete. This machine can process any computable function and includes most modern computers.

Unconfirmed: When a transaction is proposed, it is unconfirmed until the network has examined the blockchain to ensure that there are no other transactions pending involving that exact same coin. In the unconfirmed state, the transaction has not been appended to the blockchain.

Unspent Transaction Output: This refers to the amount of cryptocurrency sent to an entity, but not sent on elsewhere. These amounts are considered unspent and is the data stored in the blockchain.

UTXO: Acronym for unspent transaction output.

Volatility: The fluctuation in an asset's prices is measured by its volatility. Cryptocurrency prices are notoriously volatile compared to other assets since dramatic price shifts can happen quickly.

Wallet: A wallet is defined by a unique code, which represents its address on the blockchain. The wallet address is public, but within it are a number of private keys determining ownership of the balance and the balance itself. It can exist in software, hardware, paper or other forms.

Whale: A term used to describe extremely wealthy traders who have enough funds to manipulate the market.

Whitelist: Prior to an ICO, interested parties can sign-up/register their involvement and intent to purchase or even purchase under pre-sale conditions. The list of these parties is referred to as the whitelist.

Whitepaper: A detailed explanation of a cryptocurrency, which is designed to offer satisfactory technical information, explain the purpose of the coin and set out a roadmap for how it plans to succeed. It's designed to convince traders that it's a good choice ahead of an initial coin offering.

Zero Confirmation Transaction: Alternative phrasing for an unconfirmed transaction.

STAY AHEAD OF THE GAME

The army of cryptocurrency experts we have at finder extends all the way around the world. Our team of journalists is on top of every daily event in the cryptocurrency industry and you can be too! You just need to stay up-to-date with all the news, information, guides and comparisons that arrive on the finder website every single day. The best way to ensure you never miss a thing is to sign up for our newsletter.

Simply head to www.finder.com.au/cryptocurrency-news and follow the instructions. You will also see links to our many social channels there, which are another great way to ensure you're making the best cryptocurrency choice for you.

Do you prefer video content?

Our most recent addition to the finder cryptocurrency experience is crypto finder TV. There are a number of shows on offer, ranging from daily price analysis through to detailed interviews with the leaders in the cryptocurrency space. It's all broadcast live from finder HQ through Facebook, YouTube and more, with replays then available for those who missed it first time around.

Just make your way over to YouTube and search "crypto finder."

www.finder.com/cryptocurrency